EXPLORING HOW TEXTS WORK

Beverly Derewianka

PRIMARY ENGLISH TEACHING ASSOCIATION

Paul Jennings' story "Unhappily Ever After" is reprinted from *Quirky Tails* by kind permission of the author and Penguin Books Australia Ltd.

National Library of Australia Cataloguing-in-Publication data

Derewianka, Beverly, 1946–
Exploring How Texts Work

ISBN 0 909955 90 5

1. English language – Composition and exercises – Study and teaching (Primary). 2. Language experience approach in education.
I. Primary English Teaching Association (Australia). II. Title.

372.623044

First published March 1990
Revised impression August 1991
Reprinted February 1992
Reprinted August 1992
Reprinted April 1993
Reprinted March 1994
Reprinted November 1994
Reprinted December 1995
Reprinted January 1997
Reprinted August 1998
Copyright © Primary English Teaching Association 1990
Laura Street Newtown NSW 2042 Australia
Cover design by Greg Gaul
Edited and designed by Jeremy V. Steele
Typeset in 11 / 13 Palatino by Suzana Scurla
Printed by Australian Print Group
76 Nelson Street Maryborough Vic 3465

FOREWORD

This book has been written as a sequel to the PETA book *Writing for Life*, edited by John Collerson. *Writing for Life* has aroused a great deal of interest among teachers about how to introduce various genres into their programs. Many have started to implement the ideas presented in the book and are now feeling the need for more information about texts and how they work. The purpose of this book is to provide this sort of information in a systematic way, relating it to how certain teachers have used such information in their classrooms.

The book is based on the experiences of a group of Wollongong teachers who, over several months, trialled various ideas and approaches and looked for ways of using their developing knowledge about texts in their normal classroom practice. They were teaching in a variety of schools – Government and Catholic, rural and inner-city – most of which had a large population of students of non-English-speaking background. The teachers involved were Peter Bodycott, Dianne Dal Santo, Fran Egan, Rasheeda Flight, Bob King, Alix Mungovan and Mick Schmich. Their commitment to the project and their willingness to spend time sharing their expertise and ideas are greatly valued.

The project was based upon the work done by Professor Michael Halliday, Dr Jim Martin, Joan Rothery, Professor Fran Christie, Clare Painter, Professor Gunther Kress and others in developing a functional model of language for use in schools. Their research is gratefully acknowledged. The project also drew on the publications of similar studies being conducted by the Studies Directorate (NSW Department of Education) and the Disadvantaged Schools Program (NSW Metropolitan East Region) and thanks must go to all involved for their inspiration and support.

Chapter	Curriculum Context	Focus Activity	Text Features	Language Highlight
2 Year 2	Botanical Excursion: Telling What Happened	Planning/ Programming	Recount	What Is a Text? (Genre/Register)
3 Year 5	Craft Theme: How to Make Things from Scraps	Using Oral Language for Learning	Instructions	Differences between Oral and Written Language
4 Year 4	Writing a Narrative: What Makes a Good Story?	Exploring Narratives	Narrative	Different Types of Processes
5 Year 3	Communications: The Telephone	Modelling a Report	Information Report	Different Ways of Knowing
6 Year 3	Communications: How Does the Phone System Work?	Joint Construction of a Text	Explanation	More on Oral and Written Language
7 Year 5	History: Was Ned Kelly Guilty or Innocent?	Conferencing and Evaluation	Argument	The Politics of Language

CONTENTS

Foreword   v

How To Read This Book   1

1   A Functional Approach to Language   3

2   Recounts   10

3   Instructions   23

4   Narratives   32

5   Information Reports   47

6   Explanations   57

7   Arguments   71

    Postscript   82

    Appendix   84

    References   88

HOW TO READ THIS BOOK

The opening chapter takes a quick look at some of the ideas about language theory and classroom practice underlying this book. It would be a good idea to at least skim through this chapter first, and then return to it after reading a couple of later chapters.

All the later chapters employ the same format. Each looks at a particular genre and at how knowledge about the genre and its typical language features might be used in the classroom. The chapters are organised into four distinct but related sections.

1. Curriculum Context

The description of a unit of work in this section is based on the experiences of practising classroom teachers and is intended to demonstrate how we can draw upon our knowledge about language in planning and implementing the curriculum.

2. Focus Activity

One activity within the unit of work is described in greater detail to illustrate how we can create and exploit opportunities for developing in the class an explicit awareness of language and how it works (e.g. during conferencing, shared book or the joint construction of texts).

3. Summary of Text Features

This section looks at the typical language patterns to be found in the genre in question. It is meant as a teacher resource and can be used as a handy reference when programming. *There is no intention that the information included should be "taught" to the class out of context. Rather it provides a starting point for the teacher, who can then be in a more informed position to guide the children towards an understanding of how texts achieve their purposes most effectively.* It is up to the teacher to draw upon this knowledge as the need arises (e.g. in planning, in class discussions, in conferencing, in evaluation). The extent to which the class develops an explicit and shared understanding of how different texts work must be judged by the teacher in relation to the needs of the particular children in the class.

In this section terms from traditional grammar have been used for the sake of familiarity. They are accompanied by functional terms in brackets, although these may not always be exactly equivalent.

4. Language Highlight

Apart from the language patterns associated with particular genres, we can also identify other aspects of language which are not specific to any one genre. Some of these insights into how language functions have been included at the end of each chapter for those interested in knowing more about language. Again, this information is provided for the benefit of the teacher, not as teaching material (although, at the appropriate moment, some of these insights may prove interesting and useful for certain students).

1 : A FUNCTIONAL APPROACH TO LANGUAGE

It is often said that children, as they use language, are constantly

> learning language
> learning through language, and
> learning about language.

We never stop **learning language** – from the babbling of babies to the voracious preschool years, from our early encounters with print and our first attempts at writing through to the secondary textbooks and essays, and then beyond to the new demands of adulthood, where we still continue to learn and refine the language needed in every new situation in which we find ourselves.

And it is now widely recognised that we **learn through language** – that language is absolutely central in the learning process. Our perception of the world is constructed through language, and it is through language that we are able to interact with others in our world. In schools, we could virtually say that "language **is** the curriculum".

But what of **learning *about* language**? As we use language, we develop a relatively unconscious, implicit understanding of how it works. A functional approach to language attempts to make these commonsense understandings explicit. Once they have been brought out into the open, we can use them to help us in the classroom.

WHAT IS A FUNCTIONAL APPROACH TO LANGUAGE ?

A functional approach looks at how language enables us to **do** things – to share information, to enquire, to express attitudes, to entertain, to argue, to get our needs met, to reflect, to construct ideas, to order our experience and make sense of the world. It is concerned with how people use real language for real purposes. At the heart of a functional model of language is an emphasis on **meaning** and on how language is involved in the construction of meaning. It sees language as a resource for making meaning.

A functional approach to language is not concerned with a set of rules which prescribe correct and incorrect usage. Language in real life is not a complete, ideal system conforming to neat, pre-determined categories. Language is dynamic and ever-evolving. **We** develop language to satisfy our needs in society. Language is functional when it fulfils those needs effectively.

WHAT ARE THE ADVANTAGES OF A FUNCTIONAL APPROACH TO LANGUAGE?

§ A functional model of language complements modern classroom practice based on **holistic** approaches to language teaching and learning.

§ Like Whole Language, it is interested above all in **meaning**, not in empty conventions.

§ Because meaning is found within a text as a **whole**, a functional model of language describes how language operates at the text level, not at the level of individual words and sentences in isolation.

§ A functional approach to language stresses how meanings are made **in conjunction with other people**. This strongly supports the small groupwork and conferencing practices of today's classrooms.

§ It is concerned with **real** language used by real people – not schoolbook exercises contrived purely to teach some point of grammar, or reading texts devised to teach some aspect of reading.

§ It is not interested in simply teaching language for the sake of teaching language. Rather, it demonstrates how language operates in **all areas of the curriculum**.

§ In primary classrooms today, there is an emphasis on writing for specific **purposes**. A functional approach to language attempts to show how texts can most effectively achieve these purposes.

§ Children today are also encouraged to write with a particular **audience** in mind. A functional model describes how texts will vary according to whom you are addressing and how distant that audience is.

§ Perhaps most importantly, the knowledge of language provided by a functional model helps us to identify what children's strengths are and to make **clear and positive** suggestions as to **how** they might make their texts more effective, instead of vague, superficial comments or mere corrections of spelling and punctuation.

§ If children have an explicit knowledge of what language resources are available, they are in a better position to make **informed choices** when developing texts of their own.

HOW MIGHT YOU USE A FUNCTIONAL APPROACH TO LANGUAGE IN THE CLASSROOM?

A functional approach to language does not advocate teaching about language by handing down prescriptive recipes. Rather it is concerned with providing information about the development of effective texts for particular purposes, and providing it at the point of need within the context of real, purposeful language use. A functional model of language can be drawn upon during classroom activities based on a "process" or "whole language" philosophy – wherever children are engaged in the construction of texts and opportunities are created for explicit discussion of these texts. Such opportunities might occur, for example, during the modelling of a text, during a shared book activity, during the construction of a class text, or during a conferencing session. Sometimes these opportunities can be programmed, sometimes they may be spontaneous. They can occur at the whole class, small group, or individual level.

Many teachers have found it useful to develop in the class "a language for talking about language". These shared understandings about text, reflected in the shared terminology used by the class, allow for a more productive use of time. They can be built up through group reflection on the language as it is used, starting with questions like these.

What do you think we might use this sort of a text for in our society?

What could we call it?

Remember when we were writing Explanations? Why is this text different from an Explanation?

Look at the beginning of the text. What do you think the writer is doing here? What does the beginning of this text tell the reader?

Is it the same as the beginning of a Report?

What name could we give this sort of a beginning? What about a term such as "orientation" to remind us that it is setting the scene?

Which words link up the text and show us when the actions took place? We could call these "linking words".

Thus the children are guided towards making explicit the knowledge they already have about texts. This shared knowledge and terminology, combined with the insights contributed by the teacher, then becomes a resource they can draw on in their subsequent discussions of texts.

The teachers you will meet in the chapters of this book decided to trial a variety of activities which would allow for the growth of shared under-standings about texts. In particular, they drew on the curriculum cycle outlined in the support documents for *Writing K-12* and the NSW Disadvantaged Schools Program materials (see **References**). The cycle they jointly developed, described in the following pages, provided a context for language exploration while the children were using language for real purposes in a variety of curriculum areas.

CURRICULUM CYCLE

Preparation

• Identify the major understandings and abilities to be developed in the unit of work you are preparing (e.g. finding and organising information about transport, putting forward an argument on conservation, telling a horror story). Specific topics can be negotiated with the children during the unit, and you might also negotiate some end product (e.g. big book, letter to press/government minister) to provide a goal the children can work towards and an audience they can reach out to.

• Decide which genre (or genres) would be appropriate to develop these understandings/abilities (e.g. Report, Argument, Narrative). This becomes the language focus of the unit.

• Plan a number of activities to familiarise the children with the subject-matter and the genre, ranging from hands-on, exploratory, oral activities through to more reflective, written activities.

• Locate sample texts in the chosen genre to use for immersion and modelling. Read them carefully beforehand to become familiar with their features.

Note
It's important to know how well children can already use the genre. If you are uncertain, you may find it helpful to ask them to write a text "cold",

using the genre in question, so that strengths and weaknesses become apparent and they can observe how their texts improve as they progress through the unit.

Your assessment of the children's proficiency in the genre at this stage may well influence the subsequent phases of the unit – for instance:

- if the genre is relatively unfamiliar to most of the children, the class may need to develop common basic understandings about it as a whole group

- if the class has worked previously with the genre, it may help to look at specific aspects, e.g. how to write an effective beginning

- if the children demonstrate quite different levels of proficiency, it may be a good idea to work with groups on different aspects.

Modelling

If children are to write in a particular genre, they first need to become familiar with its purpose and features through immersion in the genre and by exploring sample texts.

- Introduce a model of the genre to the class (e.g. using the OHP). Choose or compose a text which is similar to the one to be written later as a joint construction by the class.

- Discuss the purposes for which we use this type of text in our society (e.g. the purpose of a Recount is to tell what happened).

- With the class, identify how the text is structured. Each genre has a distinctive set of stages which help it to achieve its purpose. These stages make up its **schematic structure**. (The schematic structure of a Recount, for example, consists of an orientation which sets the scene, followed by a series of events which tell what happened.) It's a good idea to look at a copy of the model text with its stages clearly marked, and to give the children a photocopy of this for later reference.

- Discuss the function of each stage. (For instance, the function of the orientation of a Recount is to let the reader know who was involved, when and where the events took place, and any other information necessary to understand the events which follow.)

Note
§ Some teachers might introduce the features of a text directly to the children, while others might prefer, through careful guidance and question-

ing, to help the children discover the features themselves (in which case the class may need to examine several examples of the same genre).

§ During the modelling phase you may wish to compare a successful text with one which has not achieved its purpose, asking the children to work out why.

§ It may also be interesting to compare the structure and stages of this genre with one previously examined.

§ Model texts can be commercially published ones, texts written previously by students, or texts written by the teacher.

§ In the modelling phase you can also refer to language features other than the structure of the text, but it's probably most helpful to start with a picture of the text as a whole.

Joint Construction

Before children write independent texts, it is useful for them to participate in the group writing of a text in the chosen genre. A text may be jointly constructed by the whole class, by a small group, or by a teacher and child during conferencing.

• *Researching the topic.* Before writing, we need to make sure we have something to write about. We often need to research the topic. The type of research we do will depend on the genre we plan to use, e.g.

Report: observing/reading/making notes/watching video

Argument: discussion/interviews/finding evidence

Narrative: brainstorming/silent contemplation.

At this stage you may find it necessary to work with the children on researching skills (e.g. use of library, locating information in a book, note-making).

• *Pooling information.* As well as demonstrating what form the final product may take, the joint construction of a text also demonstrates the process involved in writing a text. So, as the children build up their data banks and start pooling their ideas and information, they may need guidance in organising their jottings through the use of matrix charts, columns, headings, flowcharts, and so on.

• *Revising structure.* It may be helpful at this stage to revise the schematic structure of the genre (e.g. by referring to model texts).

• *Jointly constructing a text.* Let the children contribute the information and ideas while you act as guide, asking questions and making suggestions about the structuring of the text. Scribe the text yourself so that the children can concentrate on the meanings they are creating. When it's complete, give them each a copy as a further model.

• *Assessing the children's progress.* Some children may be keen to try an independent text, while others may feel they need further modelling. So at this stage flexibility may be needed, with different groups working on different tasks.

Independent Construction of Text

Having read and examined specimen texts in the chosen genre, and having had the experience of jointly constructing a similar text, many children may now choose to write their own texts on a related topic.

• Each child, possibly with your guidance, chooses a topic. For instance, if you've already modelled a text on "How to care for your dog", a child might choose to write a similar text on caring for cats, or goldfish, or tortoises.

• The children write their drafts, referring to models.

• Each child consults with you and/or peer(s), receiving comments on what he or she has achieved (in the light of built-up, shared knowledge about the genre) and suggestions for changes to help the text achieve its purpose more effectively.

• You may find that conferencing about drafts reveals a need for more modelling and joint construction.

• Editing and publishing the children's texts are optional final steps.

Public conferencing of some of the children's texts (in a constructive way and with each writer's permission) can encourage discussion of more detailed language features, just as shared reading of children's texts can give further opportunities for modelling the genre.

Children eventually reach the point where they can undertake writing the genre quite independently. Indeed they may choose to do so in free-choice writing sessions, for contract work or for projects. When they have gained control of the basic features, they may move on to exploit the genre more creatively.

2 : RECOUNTS

Curriculum Context

LOOKING AT PLANTS IN OUR NEIGHBOURHOOD

Alix was pleased with the progress her second graders were making in writing. They came from a wide variety of ethnic backgrounds and when they entered school they were quite unused to hearing and using English. Since kindergarten they had been immersed in texts and been encouraged to "have a go" at writing. They clearly enjoyed writing and most of them produced a prolific number of drafts each term. Every day they drew pictures, labelled them, and wrote their observations and comments about the things and events surrounding them:

This is my dog.	[Labelling]
My dog is big.	[Observation]
I like my dog.	[Comment]

Alix had noticed that some of the children were starting to move on to more sustained texts:

DINOSAURS 20489
on Wednesday
aoouClass Went
to The Museum
and We Siou and
Tyranposaurus Rex
and We Siou bones.
and Went Si
Serafino

On Wednesday our class
went to the museum
and we saw Tyrannosaurus
Rex and we saw bones.

Alix decided to do some work on Recounts with them. In their next unit of work on plants in the local neighbourhood, they were to look at the various types of plants that grew in different areas. As part of the unit, they would be going on an excursion to observe and compare plantlife on the beach, at the steelworks and in the rainforest. This would provide an excellent opportunity to write Recounts of their trip and what they found out. These Recounts could be written in the form of letters to their families telling them what happened on the excursion, thus providing the children with an appreciative audience with whom to share their writing. (Alix also saw this as a useful strategy to inform parents of school activities and to involve them in reading with their children at home.)

Early in the week, Alix made the children more aware of how we are constantly using Recounts in our everyday lives. She started by asking them to tell her what they did on the weekend. She felt it would be useful to develop a shared terminology when referring to this type of text, so she introduced the term "Recount":

> "When we tell someone what happened, we can call it a Recount. You've just given me a Recount of what you did on the weekend. Here's another example of a Recount *(shows the class a newspaper story on the OHP)*. Can you think of some more examples of Recounts?"

During the week some children from 4th class visited Alix's classroom and in small groups shared Recounts that they had written of the school camp they had just been on.

Over the next few days Alix read the children a number of different types of Recounts which she wrote out on butcher's paper and pinned around the room as models. She then suggested that they might like to write a Recount of the coming excursion.

On the day of the excursion, she took along the school's videocamera. She filmed the children at the seaside looking at the spinifex grass and the gnarled ti-trees, then at the steelworks examining the patches of grass among the concrete and the few hardy trees covered in coal dust, and finally marvelling at the lush vegetation of the nearby rainforest. The children assumed the role of "apprentice botanists", taking field notes and making sketches to record the types of plants they saw and where they were found.

On their return to school, they shared their observations in the form of oral Recounts. They then took great delight in watching themselves on the TV as they relived the excursion on video. The video served as a memory-jogger, reminding them of details which might otherwise have gone unrecorded. At various points Alix put the video on "pause" and constructed a flowchart of the stages of the excursion, drawing a sequence of pictures of the locations visited and the plants found at each one.

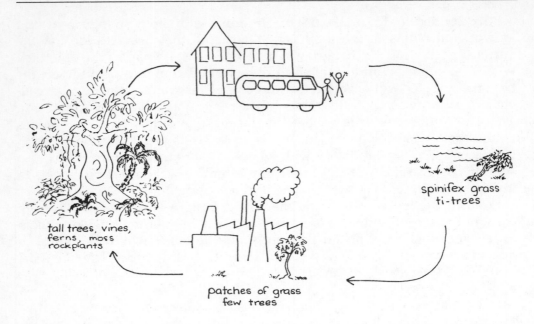

spinifex grass
ti-trees

tall trees, vines,
ferns, moss
rockplants

patches of grass
few trees

The flowchart gave the children a visual idea of the sequence, and served as a prompt for them when it came to constructing a class Recount of the excursion. Alix guided them in writing a text telling what happened during the outing and what they discovered at the various sites by asking questions like these.

Where did we go first?

What sort of plants did we find there?

What did they look like?

Why do you think they were twisted?

How could we write that down?

When they had finished, Alix suggested that they might start off by letting their readers know a bit of background information, like

> **who** took part in the excursion
>
> **why**
>
> **when** it happened.

The session finished with a brief review of how the class had structured their Recount – an orientation followed by a series of events.

The next day the children tried writing their own Recounts of the excursion for their families, referring to the flowchart on the board and their personal field notes and sketches. Because they were writing about experiences which

Alix had shared, she found conferencing much easier. She was aware of the sorts of meanings the children were trying to construct and could help them shape these up into a text.

Dear Mum and Dad,

On Thursday 2.2 went on an excursion to observe plants.

First we went to Port Kembla Beach. There were not many plants because of the salt and the sand. Then we got back on the bus.

Next we went to the steelworks. We sat on a hill and observed the plants. We saw bushes and grass. Not many plants grow because of the pollution.

We got back on the bus and went to Mt. Keira rainforest. We got off the bus and ate our little lunch in the clearing area. We saw many different types of plants and trees. We saw wattle trees, tall trees, thin trees and rock plants.

After that we got back on the bus and went back to school. We arrived at school at 12 o'clock. Then we went into school and talked about our excursion.

We had GREAT fun!!!!

Aneta

Focus Activity

PLANNING/PROGRAMMING

The first stage of any curriculum cycle like the one just outlined takes place outside the classroom, when the teacher starts to plan the learning experiences that the children will engage in over the following weeks.

When programming the unit on "Plants in our neighbourhood", Alix took into consideration such factors as:

- her knowledge of the children in her class – their previous experiences, what they could already do, what they needed assistance with, what their interests were, etc.

- the sorts of understandings about the world which various syllabus documents suggested, resulting in focus questions like:

    What are the characteristics of different types of plants?
    Why do certain plants grow in particular environments?
    How are they affected by their environment?
    How might we classify plants?

On this basis, she identified an appropriate genre to concentrate on in the unit. While she felt that the subject matter lent itself to the writing of a

Report on the different types of local plants, she decided that a Recount of the excursion would be equally appropriate and would match the children's current abilities and interests more closely.

From previous experience, Alix feels it is preferable to work on only one genre within a unit of work (although she will often refer to other genres that the class are familiar with in order to compare and contrast their features). The selection of the genre usually arises naturally out of the focus of the unit. A unit on "How a camera works" would automatically lead to the writing of an Explanation; a unit on "Should woodchipping be banned?" would most likely end up as an Argument or Discussion; a unit on "Making kites" could logically include the writing of Instructions; and so on. By working within a context which calls for the use of a particular genre, the children are able to relate the genre to its purpose.

Having decided on the topic of the unit and a relevant genre, Alix then goes on to devise a number of activities aimed at developing certain under-standings about the topic and at achieving a degree of control over the genre in question. While she sees her planning as providing an overall guide, she always ensures there is room for flexibility. With the younger children she usually begins orally with lots of hands-on, problem-solving activities to encourage them to engage with the topic and to familiarise them with the subject matter. She then moves towards the use of written texts and, at appropriate points, weaves in such strategies as modelling the genre and jointly constructing texts (see **Focus Activity,** pp. 34, 50, 58). The ultimate goal of the unit is usually the independent writing of a text in the chosen genre.

Alix finds that her greatest problem at the planning stage is locating appropriate texts to use as models which the children can then refer to and read in silent reading sessions. She usually enlists the help of the librarian, who supplies the class with relevant books, but finds that she often needs to write her own model texts. Gradually she is building up a library of short, sufficiently simple (though well-written) texts covering a variety of genres, including ones written by herself and by the children, as well as those she keeps collecting from her everyday reading.

Summary of Text Features

RECOUNTS (What we did/What took place)

In a Recount we reconstruct past experience. A Recount is the unfolding of a sequence of events over time. We are using language to keep the past alive and help us to interpret experience.

Purpose

To tell what happened.

Types

Personal Recount – retelling of an activity that the writer/speaker has been personally involved in (e.g. oral anecdote, diary entry).

Factual Recount – recording the particulars of an incident (e.g. report of a science experiment, police report, news report, historical account).

Imaginative Recount – taking on an imaginary role and giving details of events (e.g. a day in the life of a Roman slave; how I invented ...).

Text Organisation

The focus is on a sequence of events, all of which relate to a particular occasion.

The Recount generally begins with an
> **orientation**

giving the reader/listener the background information needed to understand the text (i.e. *who* was involved, *where* it happened, *when* it happened).

Then the Recount unfolds with a
> **series of events**

ordered in a chronological sequence.

At various stages there may be some
> **personal comment**

on the incident (e.g. We had a wonderful time).

Language Features

General

• Specific participants (Mrs Brady, our dog, the shopkeeper).

• Use of simple past tense (she smiled, it barked, he pointed).

• Use of action verbs *[material processes]* (went, climbed, ate).

• Use of linking items to do with time (on Wednesday, then, at the same time, next, later, before).

• Details irrelevant to the purpose of the text should be avoided.

Personal Recount

• Use of first person pronouns (I, we).

SAMPLE TEXT: RECOUNT

Text Organisation

Language Features

Furious Pace in Hockey Finals

orientation

Spectators were treated to a feast of fast hockey on the weekend when the South Coast Women's Hockey Association staged four grand finals at Kiama.

when?
who?
what?
where?

The highlight of the day was the Division One grand final between Gerringong and minor premiers Warilla which was a hard, fast game, with the speed of the young Gerringong team proving the difference on the day.

events

Warilla stormed the Gerringong circle from the start of the game but the Gerringong defence held out and then took the attack to Warilla's 25 yard line through speedy centre forward Jenny Miller.

action verbs/ past tense

After a period of midfield play Warilla's right inner Mandy Smith broke away but again met solid Gerringong defence.

linking words to do with time

Gerringong continued to move the ball quickly and just five minutes before half-time, Gerringong's left wing Michelle Cooper finally latched on to the ball and put it between the posts after having narrowly missed connecting with a shot several minutes earlier.

specific participants

Lake Times, 20 September 1989

- Personal responses to the events can be included, particularly at the end.
- Details are often chosen to add interest or humour.

Factual Recount

- Use of third person pronouns (he, she, it, they).
- Details are usually selected to help the reader reconstruct the activity or incident accurately.
- Sometimes the ending describes the outcome of the activity (e.g. in a science experiment).
- Mention of personal feelings is probably not appropriate.
- Details of time, place and manner may need to be precisely stated (e.g. at *2.35 pm*, between *Johnson St* and *Park Rd*, the man drove at *80 kph*).
- Descriptive details may also be required to provide precise information (e.g. a man with a *red shirt, brown shoes* and *long hair*, weighing *75 kilos* and approximately *189 cm* tall).
- The passive voice may be used (e.g. the beaker *was filled* with water).
- It may be appropriate to include explanations and justifications.

Imaginative Recount

- Usually written in the first person.
- It may be appropriate to include personal reactions.

Language Highlight

WHAT IS A TEXT?

In this book we are looking at texts and how they work. A text is any meaningful stretch of language – oral or written. But of course not all texts are the same, and a functional model of language tries to describe the ways in which they differ. It is interested in what language **choices** are available within any particular situation, and in which choices are more likely to result in an **effective** text which achieves its purpose.

One factor which accounts for differences in texts is the **purpose** for which the text is being used. Texts are structured in different ways to achieve their purposes. The purpose of Instructions, for example, is to tell someone how to do or make something. The structure of such a text would typically move through the following stages:

- stating the goal (i.e. what's to be made or done)

- outlining any materials or equipment needed

- detailing the steps to be taken.

The purpose of a Recount, on the other hand, is to tell what happened. To achieve its purpose, the text will move through a different set of stages:

- an orientation letting the reader know who is involved, where, when, etc.

- the retelling of a series of events in chronological sequence.

We can refer to this as the **schematic structure** of the Recount genre.

When we look at how the schematic structure of a text helps it to achieve its purpose, we are considering its **genre**. (The term "genre" is used here to refer to particular text-types, not to traditional varieties of literature.) The genre of a text is partly determined by the **culture** in which the text is used, since different cultures achieve their purposes through language in different ways.

But texts differ not only in terms of their purpose (and therefore overall structure). They also differ according to the particular **situation** in which they are being used. The type of language used in a text will depend on:

- the relationship between the participants: speaker/listener; writer/ reader (i.e. the **tenor**)

- the subject-matter of the text (i.e. the **field**)

- the channel of communication being used: written or spoken (i.e. the **mode**).

These three factors together determine the **register** of the text.

We could describe the relationship between the genre and register of a text in terms of the diagram on the facing page.

A functional model of language tries to describe the sort of language which is typical of different types of situation. There are no hard and fast rules, but we can predict in a general way the patterns of language which we would probably find in various situations. For example, let's contrast the language patterns found in the following texts.

TEXT A

Customer: G'day, Maggie. Um, let's see .... Got any dinner rolls?
Assistant: Sorry love, all out of them.
Customer: What about ...
Assistant: Do you want these instead?

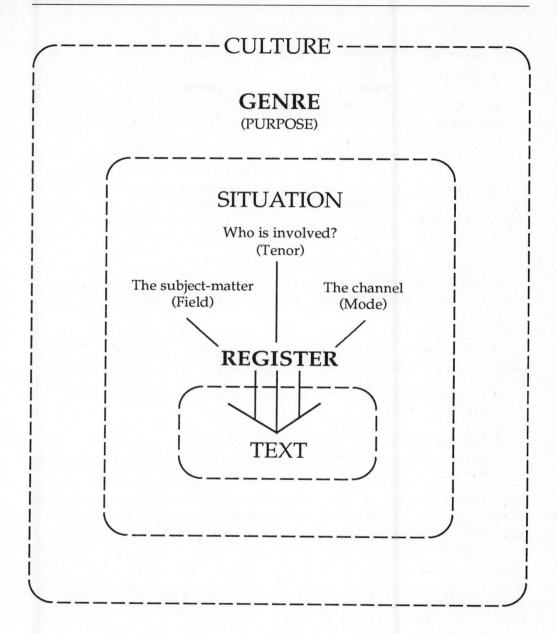

Customer: I suppose they're okay. What – how much are they?
Assistant: Just the same I think.
Customer: Okay, give us half a dozen.
Assistant: Righto. Here you go, love. That's $1.20.
Customer: Thanks. See you.
Assistant: Yeah.

TEXT B

The Rough Maidenhair fern is a creeping monomorphic wintergreen mountain fern which belongs to the *Adiantum* family. It is a native of Asia, southern Australia and New Zealand. It is found in mountainous areas where it grows in cool crevices. Like all maidenhair ferns it is of delicate appearance and the young fronds are a bright pink colour when unfurling.

In these two texts, both the genre and the register differ. The purpose of the first text is to purchase something, so its genre is that of a "shopping exchange". To achieve its purpose of buying goods, the text goes through a number of stages:

- greeting
- query about availability of the goods
- apology and counter-offer
- query about cost/requesting of goods
- compliance with request
- leave-taking.

The purpose of Text B is to give information about a type of plant. Its genre is that of an Information Report. It goes through different stages in achieving its purpose:

- general classification statement
- description (location, habitat, appearance).

So the overall structure of the texts varies according to their purpose (genre).

But we can look more closely at the language of the texts and see how they also vary in terms of their register. The language features are quite different because the registers are different, i.e. the situations in which they were produced differed in terms of tenor, field and mode.

Tenor

The tenor of a text will depend on the roles of the participants and their relationship, e.g.

- how well they know each other
- their ages
- their relative status
- how they feel towards each other.

In Text A the speakers are old acquaintances – the shopkeeper at a corner store and a regular customer. Both are adults of approximately equal status engaged in an everyday, informal exchange. Many of the language features of the text reflect this relationship, e.g.

- the use of language expressing opinions, feelings ("I suppose they're okay")
- the use of first and second person pronouns ("I", "you")
- the use of intimate forms of address ("Maggie", "love")
- the use of colloquial terms ("Righto. Here you go")
- the use of abbreviated sentences ("[Have you] Got any dinner rolls?").

In Text B the relationship between the writer and reader is one of expert to expert (or at least informed apprentice). The writer and reader are not personally known to each other, and so here we find a neutral tenor:

- no expression of personal feelings and emotion
- no use of personal pronouns
- a certain formality.

Field

The field of a situation refers to "what is going on" – the doings and happenings, who or what is involved in them (the **participants**), and the circumstances in which they are taking place (where and when). Basically we could say it is the subject-matter of the text.

In Text A the field is shopping, and in particular buying bread rolls. There is reference to specific participants ("dinner rolls", "half a dozen") and other words related to shopping ("How much ...", "give us ..."). The field in Text B, however, is Science – more particularly, Botany. The text refers to generalised phenomena and abstract concepts ("mountainous areas", "all maidenhair ferns") and employs technical terms ("monomorphic", "*Adiantum*"). (See **Language Highlight**, p. 55.)

Mode

In basic terms, mode deals with the channel of communication – with:

- how distant the speaker/writer is from the listener/reader in both time and space (e.g. a face-to-face conversation as opposed to a book written for an audience the author will never meet)
- the extent to which the language accompanies the action going on (as in an oral commentary on a cricket match) or is distanced from the action (as in a newspaper article written after the match).

Text A is a transcript of a spoken conversation. It has the hesitancies, backtracking and interruptions characteristic of spoken language as the participants engage in constructing meanings jointly. It also contains references to the immediate physical situation ("Do you want *these* instead?").

Text B, however, is written and the writer has had time to carefully construct and organise the text. Because the writer is physically distanced from the reader, all the meanings must be included in the text itself – it must be self-sufficient. It also concentrates meanings into compact, dense language ("a creeping monomorphic wintergreen mountain fern") – a typical feature of many written texts. (See **Language Highlight,** p. 62.)

We could say then that texts vary according to their **genre** (purpose) and their **register** (tenor, field and mode). The genre will determine the overall structuring of the text and the register will determine the language patterns found within the text.

3 : INSTRUCTIONS

Curriculum Context

HOW TO MAKE THINGS FROM SCRAPS

Fran is a firm believer in the idea that language is an integral part of all areas of the curriculum. So, when she started to plan a craft unit with Year 5, she decided it would be useful to look in some detail at the instructional texts they would be using. The children were already quite familiar with Instructions in their everyday life – who gives them, for what purpose, and to whom. But they had had little experience with writing instructional texts.

Her first step was to discuss with the children the reasons why we use Instructions and to immerse them in examples of the genre. They accomplished numerous everyday tasks following simple oral and written Instructions. Other activities made them more aware of various features of the genre, e.g.

- text sequencing games, where Fran would take an instructional text, cut it up into segments and ask a group to put it together again, explaining why they made the decisions they did

- "barrier games", in which one group was given a map, diagram or drawing and had to give Instructions to another group on the other side of a divider, with enough detail to enable the second group to replicate the original.

After the games they discussed the problems they had had and what they had learned about giving Instructions.

At a later stage Fran helped small groups to write instruction cards for all the equipment used by pupils in the school – the video, the computer, the tape recorder, the photocopier – so that the children could operate these machines independently.

As they discovered features of instructional texts, they would note them on a sheet of butcher's paper on the wall:

- *You have to use simple language or people mightn't understand you.*

- *Many instruction texts have a list of materials at the beginning.*

- *Each step has to follow in a certain order.*

- *It makes it easier to follow if the steps are numbered.*

- *You have to be very precise when giving instructions or things will go wrong.*

- *You have to give a lot of detail, because the reader can't see what to do.*

- *Diagrams make it easier to follow instructions.*

- *It is helpful if you include a diagram or photo of the finished product so that people can picture where they are heading.*

- *At certain points you can put in warnings or hints.*

After several sessions in which they had used and analysed instructional texts, the children were motivated to write one for themselves. So Fran provided cardboard, wool, paste, scissors, cellophane, paint, material, string, etc. and asked them to form groups and create anything which appealed to their imagination. As they worked, they were to take notes on the materials used and how they went about the construction.

As each group completed their creation, they wrote up Instructions outlining the steps involved, referring to their notes, previous model texts, and the list of features the class had compiled. These Instructions were then passed on to another group who attempted to follow them. A lively class discussion followed, during which each group pointed out the inadequacies of the texts which they had been given. The children ended up with a keen appreciation of the need for detail and precision in instructional texts.

As a final activity, Fran asked the children as individuals to write an instructional text for a class book entitled "Rainy Day Suggestions", which would be donated to the school library.

Focus Activity

USING ORAL LANGUAGE FOR LEARNING

Oral language often tends to be overlooked when programming. Fran, however, is very conscious of the important role oral language plays in the learning process and always plans for the children to have opportunities to come to an understanding of the content through oral language, gradually moving them towards the written mode.

It is through **oral** language that we have a chance to interact directly with others and

- to try out ideas
- to hypothesise
- to ask questions
- to share information
- to make mistakes and change our minds
- to start to make connections
- to give suggestions and commands
- to get immediate feedback.

Ben: How am I supposed to put this together?
Ellen: What if .... Well, what I'd do is ... you just tape it up like that and then just cut around it so it doesn't come off.
Ben: Yeah! And then I could ... no, that wouldn't work.
John: Yes it would. Look, you'd just have to cut it there.

Talking enables us to pursue and explore our purposes with a speed and ease that we can never achieve with written language. Because we use oral language to come to grips with new ideas, our talk will usually be "first draft" – lots of hesitations, unfinished sentences, tentative queries, vague expressions and random offerings. This "give-and-take" language is particularly to be valued as it allows us to formulate new understandings.

Written language, on the other hand, tends to be more highly structured, more explicit, less interactive. Because it traps our thoughts in print on the page, it allows us to organise and consolidate our thinking, to reflect on our understandings, and through this sustained reflection to make new connections.

Because of their different functions, spoken and written language have quite different forms (see **Language Highlight**, p. 28). Fran is aware of this, and as the children are engaged in making their craft items, she circulates around the room, *talking* with them in a way that starts them thinking about how they might express themselves when they *write up* their Instructions.

Fran: What did you do first?

Brad: I got a sock.

Fran A real long sock, like a footy sock?

Brad: Yeah. And then I put some paper ....

Fran: What did you do to the paper first?

Brad: I scrunched it up ... then I put on the hair.

Fran: What did you use for hair?

Brad: Bits of wool. And then the eyes.

Fran: You've used buttons for the eyes, haven't you? Tell me how you did the mouth.

Brad: Well I got some cellophane – red cellophane – and cut it out and stuck it on.

Fran: What did you stick it with?

Brad: Well first I used sticky tape but that didn't work so I tried glue.

Fran: It's looking great – what could you call it?

Brad: I think I'll call it a Grug.

Fran is using the oral mode to help the children make the transition to a written text by getting them to express precisely the steps in their Instructions, to order these in a logical sequence, to include details, to make things clear, to develop the use of appropriate terms, and to anticipate difficulties the reader might have. Taking notes during construction is another step towards the final written text. Telling the whole class how they went about the task and the problems they encountered also helps the children to stand back from the action and start to reflect on what they did. And of course, once they are actually into writing the text, each draft will take them further from the spoken mode towards a more "written" version.

Fran has deliberately planned the unit so that the children will be able to make full use of the learning potential of the oral mode and then be guided gradually towards written expression. She has programmed so that the oral discussion, the drafting of texts and the associated reading and modelling all support each other and contribute towards the production of a successful final written text.

Summary of Text Features

INSTRUCTIONS (How something is done)

Instructions belong to a group of text-types concerned with procedures, which tell us how something is accomplished through a sequence of actions or steps. It is a very important genre in our society because it enables us to get things done, and it is equally common in the oral and written mode.

Purpose

To tell someone how to do or make something.

Examples

Recipes, science experiment or craft instructions, games rules, appliance manuals, how-to-do-it kits, directions to reach a destination.

Text Organisation

The focus of instructional texts is on a sequence of actions.

The structure is easily recognised, usually consisting of:

> **Goal** (often indicated in the main heading and/or diagram)
>
> **Materials** (listed in order of use)
>
> **Method** (steps oriented towards achieving the goal).

Each stage serves a particular function – e.g. telling us what we need, or what to do next.

The text may also include comments on the usefulness, significance, danger, fun, etc. of the activity.

Headings, subheadings, numbers, diagrams, photos, etc. are often utilised to make Instructions as clear and easy to understand as possible.

Language Features

- Generalised participants referring to a whole class of things (ingredients, utensils) as well as specific ones (the eggs).

- The reader or the person following the Instructions is referred to in a general way (one/you) or sometimes is not even mentioned at all (Draw a 10 cm line).

SAMPLE TEXT: INSTRUCTIONS

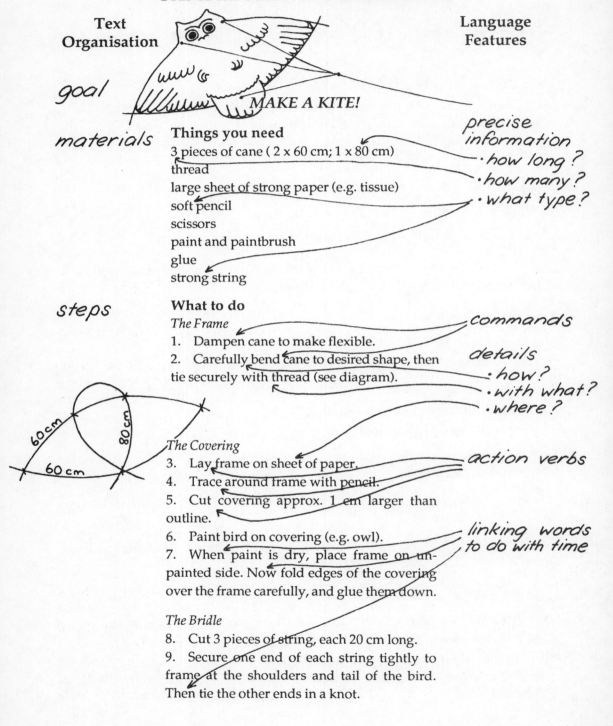

Text Organisation

Language Features

goal

MAKE A KITE!

materials

Things you need
3 pieces of cane (2 x 60 cm; 1 x 80 cm)
thread
large sheet of strong paper (e.g. tissue)
soft pencil
scissors
paint and paintbrush
glue
strong string

precise information
• *how long ?*
• *how many ?*
• *what type ?*

steps

What to do
The Frame
1. Dampen cane to make flexible.
2. Carefully bend cane to desired shape, then tie securely with thread (see diagram).

commands

details
• *how ?*
• *with what ?*
• *where ?*

60 cm
80 cm
60 cm

The Covering
3. Lay frame on sheet of paper.
4. Trace around frame with pencil.
5. Cut covering approx. 1 cm larger than outline.
6. Paint bird on covering (e.g. owl).
7. When paint is dry, place frame on unpainted side. Now fold edges of the covering over the frame carefully, and glue them down.

action verbs

linking words to do with time

The Bridle
8. Cut 3 pieces of string, each 20 cm long.
9. Secure one end of each string tightly to frame at the shoulders and tail of the bird. Then tie the other ends in a knot.

- Linking words to do with time (first, then, when).

- Mainly action verbs *[material processes]* (put, twist, hold, take).

- Tense is timeless ("what people do in general"), e.g. simple present tense (you stir, you cut, you mix).

- Detailed, factual description of participants (shape, size, colour, amount, etc.).

- Detailed information on *how* (carefully, with the knife, quickly); *where* (6 cm from the top, into the bowl, in the oven); *when* (after you have folded the napkin).

Language Highlight

DIFFERENCES BETWEEN ORAL AND WRITTEN TEXTS

Oral and written language perform different roles in our society and therefore have different features.

Oral language is mostly used in face-to-face situations, where the speakers jointly construct the meanings. Because they are in a shared context, there is often no need to include specific information in the conversation. Let's take the example of the boys in Fran's class making a pulley to send messages around the classroom.

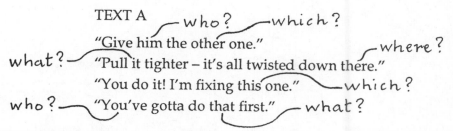

TEXT A

"Give him the other one."

"Pull it tighter – it's all twisted down there."

"You do it! I'm fixing this one."

"You've gotta do that first."

who? *which?* *where?* *what?* *who?* *what?*

This exchange would be quite meaningless to anyone who wasn't there. But the boys had no trouble understanding each other because they could see the objects referred to and were aware of the activity surrounding them.

In a written text, however, all the information has to be in the text itself because the reader is usually distant in time and space and cannot ask for clarification or extra details. When the boys came to write the first draft of their Instructions, it was certainly more explicit and structured than their spoken language, but it was hard for them to put themselves in the reader's position and to anticipate the sort of detail the reader would need.

TEXT B

Instructions to Make a Pulley

Things you need:
2 points
string
box
2 operators

Method:
Wind the string around the points.
Attach the box.
Pull the string.

When another group tried using these Instructions, they found them difficult to follow, and further conferencing between the groups was needed to produce this final version.

TEXT C

Instructions for Making a Message Pulley

Purpose: *to send messages to a friend in the classroom.*

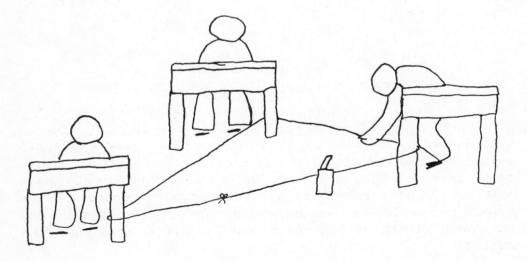

Materials:

- at least 2 points around which to loop the string, e.g. sticks (approx. 2 cm wide and 30 cm long), table legs or chair legs
- strong non-twisting string, twice the length of the distance to be covered
- at least 1 carrier of a suitable size to carry messages e.g. small, light box
- masking tape
- at least 2 operators

Method:

1. Measure the distance between the two points.
2. Cut the string to twice this distance.
3. Loop the string around the points.
4. Tie the ends of the string in a knot so that the string is stretched firmly between the points.
5. Attach the box/boxes to the string with masking tape.
6. Test the pulley out by the operator pulling one side of the string.

When you have to refer outside the text to find the meanings, as in Text A, we can call it "external reference" (or, in more technical terminology, *exophoric* reference). When all the meanings can be found within the text itself, we can call it "internal reference" (or *endophoric* reference).

Mrs Brown gave the cat some fish.

It ate them quickly.

External reference   **Internal reference**

Children, who are so accustomed to the oral mode, often "write as they speak" without realising that they cannot make assumptions about what the reader knows and doesn't know. (This is one reason why pictures are so important in children's early texts: they help to provide a context which the text can refer to – just like the cartoon above.) It takes a long time for them to be able to produce a text which can stand on its own, independent of any physical context. Teachers who are aware of the differences between oral and written language can better help children make their written texts self-sufficient.

4 : NARRATIVES

Curriculum Context

WHAT MAKES A GOOD STORY?

When I first set foot inside 4 Red's classroom, I was immediately conscious that this was a place of learning. There was a quiet buzz of activity from children engaged in a number of diverse tasks. My presence was hardly even noticed. "Mr B", as the children fondly referred to their teacher, was nowhere to be seen. Amy introduced herself to me and asked for a comment on her draft Narrative.

As I looked around I saw a group of children in an alcove watching *Fire in the Stone*. Amy explained that they had chosen to watch the video for a third time because they wanted to note down more details for the flowcharts of the story they were making. Other children were already working on the final drafts of their flowcharts – large sheets of art paper on which they had plotted the story events from the video – and were labelling the main stages of the story, using terms such as "orientation", "complication" and "resolution".

Steven and David had finished their flowcharts and were examining Colin Thiele's story on which the video was based to see how the video differed from the text. In particular they were looking at how the setting and characters were portrayed through *language* in the book, while in the video they were portrayed *visually*.

A couple of girls were busy pinning their finished texts to the wall display. A few children were sprawled on the floor reading stories and occasionally sharing special bits with the others. In the corner, three boys were earnestly conferencing about an adventure story they were jointly writing. Another group was rehearsing a "Readers' Theatre" performance, acting out the events of a story they had just finished reading. All the children in the room were totally absorbed in learning about Narratives.

Mr B came back with Daniel in tow. Daniel was from 1 Blue, 4 Red's "buddy class". After 4 Red had been reading to their buddies in 1 Blue, they had reported that many stories in the big books used in first grade were not of very high quality. So a group of 4 Red children had decided to write some "real" stories for their buddies, based on some of the literature they had been reading themselves. Daniel was to be their guinea pig, reacting to some initial drafts in terms of the appeal of the characters, the appropriateness of the illustrations, the choice of possible endings, and so on.

Daniel was whisked away by his buddies and Mr B called a few boys over to the reading corner. He had just bought the latest book by Paul Jennings – the current author hero of the class. These boys had initially been reluctant readers, so Mr B was intent on introducing them to authors who would be sure to grab their interest. His own love of books and enthusiasm for good children's literature rubbed off on the children. They sat there spellbound, revelling in Jennings' weird sense of humour. Gradually other children crept over to the reading corner. At a point where the children were tense with anticipation, Mr B stopped his reading and passed the book to one of the boys to take home. He then picked up a mystery novel by Victor Kelleher. This was to be a challenge – the plot was quite sophisticated and the language rich with evocative images and metaphor. He summarised the beginning and then started reading at a stage where the suspense was starting to build up. Once more the children were swept along into another world as visions of gigantic feline monsters stalking the dense jungle undergrowth filled their heads. When Mr B closed the book, anxious hands darted out to claim it.

Now that most children were gathered around, Mr B thought it would be a good time for them to share what they had been writing lately. The children listened intently to each others' stories and difficulties, offering encouragement and constructive comments.

It was getting close to lunchtime. Some children were keen to return to the texts they were writing, but the rest stayed for a game of "never-ending story". Together they constructed an orientation for the story, deciding on which characters would be involved, what sort of personalities they might have, what their names were, where they lived, and what sort of activity they were engaged in. Then they broke up into groups of three and invented some sort of problem or complication for the main characters to deal with. Each text was then passed to the next group, who had to resolve the current problem and pose a new one. The texts were passed on again and the pattern continued until some final climax was reached and the problems were all resolved one way or another. The texts were then read aloud, much to the delight of all involved.

The lunchtime bell had rung, but no-one appeared to have noticed.

Focus Activity

EXPLORING NARRATIVES

Peter doesn't plan a tightly structured literature program. He has an ever-evolving bank of activities to draw on as required, but finds that much of the program is generated by the class itself and he "goes with the flow". This does not mean, however, that he is a passive facilitator. He has worked hard to establish routines and expectations among the class members so that they can work responsibly and independently. He also makes sure that there will be regular opportunities each week for the children to develop a love and understanding of literature through:

- listening to stories and poems for sheer enjoyment
- choosing and reading lots of good literature of all types
- sharing their discoveries
- being introduced to a wide variety of literary texts
- writing Narratives – as a class, in groups, and as individuals
- sharing their writing and receiving feedback
- exploring the language of Narratives to see what makes for an effective story.

Peter's class regard themselves as writers – apprentice members of the authors' guild acquiring the tools of the trade. They are aware that they have a lot to learn from other writers about how to construct a story and bring it to life. Peter is teaching them to be active, critical readers, examining closely the stories they read in order to discover the ways mature writers achieve their purposes.

They are already familiar, for example, with the notion that if Narratives are to be entertaining, something out of the ordinary needs to happen – the characters have to be confronted with some sort of problem or complication, so that the reader is drawn into the plot, curious to see how the problem gets resolved. As they read together, they are constantly on the lookout for different types of complications, asking questions like these.

Why did it happen?

Who is involved?

Has the author used a fairly hackneyed type of complication or is it a fresh, unexpected one?

How is the complication introduced? In a fairly traditional way ("All of a sudden ..."), or is it cleverly blended into the story?

Is it a major complication which holds your interest throughout the story and doesn't get resolved till the end?

Or is it one of a number of minor complications, woven in to add to the suspense or complexity of the story?

Could the complication be predicted from clues left earlier by the author?

Is there in fact a complication at all? Or is this perhaps not a Narrative, but another type of story with a different purpose (e.g. a Recount)?

They also look at the different ways in which these complications are resolved.

Was it a "happy ending", or did things not work out for the best?

Was the complication left unresolved? Partially or totally?

Was the complication resolved in a simplistic, stereotyped manner ("... then I woke up" or "A fairy waved her magic wand ... "), or did the characters have to work through the problem themselves?

Was the problem resolved swiftly towards the end, or did the resolution take up most of the story?

Could you have foreseen this resolution?

They explore the different ways in which authors begin their stories.

Does the author indicate when the action took place ("Once upon a time ...", "Long ago in the Dreamtime ...", "During World War II ...")?

Is this always necessary?

How does the period in which it's set influence the storyline?

Where is the story set? Why?

By what means has the author created an impression of the setting?

What aspects of the setting are important to the development of the story?

What characters are involved?

Who is the main character? Or is there more than one main character?

How does the author prepare the reader for the coming complication?

So the children are coming to an understanding of the overall structure of a Narrative and how different authors play around with this structure. But sometimes Peter will take the class further into the text, looking at specific aspects. For instance, they might focus on the characters of a particular story and perhaps compare them with characters in different types of stories they have read, or with similar characters in stories by the same author. These are the sorts of questions they discuss.

> *How does the author build up a picture of the characters' physical appearance and personality?*
>
> *How does the author make the main character(s) interesting so that the reader will want to follow their exploits?*
>
> *What other characters are there in the story and why have they been included?*
>
> *Do any of the characters change during the story?*
>
> *What are the relations between the various characters?*
>
> *Are they "stock characters", regular inhabitants of stories (Mrs Bunny, the school bully, the wicked witch), or have they been developed into distinct individuals?*

One of the Narratives the children looked at with Peter was "Unhappily Ever After", a story from Paul Jennings' *Quirky Tails*. (For easy reference it is reprinted as an appendix to this book – see p. 84 ff.) The children each had a copy of the story, and when Peter had finished reading it, they labelled what they thought was the orientation. They discussed how there was no clear indication of when the story happened – it didn't seem to be important in this case. However, it was pretty clear from the early mention of the school tie and the strap that the location was a school. But the emphasis in the orientation was on introducing one of the characters, Albert, who was obviously preparing for an ordeal.

They felt that the main issue in the story was that Brown was a sadistic bully who enjoyed belting children, but they couldn't agree on where the complication actually began. Several opted for the part where we learn about Albert going to get a belting, while others favoured the part where Brown beats Albert.

Their disagreement could have arisen from the fact that they were being challenged by high quality literature which didn't conform to their expect-ations of a simple structure with an early major complication. In fact the major complication doesn't begin until Mr Brown is out at sea and notices that "something was wrong". The first section of the story is a lengthy orientation with a couple of minor complications, building up to the later major complication. The children's apparent confusion at this point is a useful reminder that developed narratives often play around with the schem-atic structure, and that we must always be on guard against presenting too rigid or simplistic a view of basic patterns in either adults' or children's writing.

However, all the children agreed on the resolution. They discussed how Jennings at first seems to use a hackneyed resolution – "Brown awoke and looked around" – duping us into believing it was all a nightmare. But then we become gradually aware that it was no bad dream after all, that Brown actually is in hell. The children drew parallels with similar endings by Alfred Hitchcock, and they saw the significance of the pun in the title of the book – *Quirky Tails*. They even noticed how the twist in the ending had been foreshadowed in the title of the story ("Unhappily Ever After") – itself a play on the typical fairytale resolution.

After discussing the resolution, they decided that despite its "quirkiness" Jennings' story was much like a moral tale, with the "baddy" being punished for his evil doings. Peter picked up on this observation the following day by bringing in an illustrated version of Dante's *Inferno* and showing how Jennings' story echoed the Italian classic, where Dante was rowed into the descending depths of hell and saw visions of people condemned to suffer for greed, gluttony, cruelty and so on, by eternally enduring punishments similar to their own sin.

Because the personalities of the characters were central to the story, Peter decided to spend some time looking at characterisation. The children in pairs first circled all of the bits of the text which contributed to a picture of the physical appearance of the characters. They found that in the first part of the story there were several mentions of Albert's clothing ("He wore the school uniform of short pants, blue shirt and tie. His socks had fallen down again") and his size ("The small figure ..."). Mr Brown on the other hand was a balding man, dressed in "a three-piece suit with a natty little vest", who "towered over Albert." They noticed that at the end of the story clothing and size were cleverly used to indicate that Albert and Mr Brown had swapped places. A shrunken Brown "was wearing short pants. And his socks were hanging down around his shoes. He was dressed in the school uniform." He was confronted by "a huge Jenkins" who wore "a three-piece suit with a natty little vest."

Then the children underlined the bits which seemed to say something about the personality of the characters. When they pooled their findings, Albert came across as the frightened victim with whom child readers could identify ("Albert's stomach leapt up and down ..."; "... the helpless, shaking child"), but who nevertheless was truthful and courageous ("He didn't beg, he didn't cry. He just stood there"). By contrast Mr Brown was drawn as the uncaring villain ("He would find some excuse to whack Albert – he always did"; "Let the little beggar suffer"), who "frowned" and "rushed" and "grabbed" and "shrieked".

From their analysis of the text, the children could see that the image of the characters was not created simply through the use of individual words such as adjectives, but was an overall impression which embraced what the characters did and thought and said and felt.

As well as stories by professional writers, Peter shares his own writing with the class, commenting on what he has achieved, any difficulties and frustrations he is having, the decisions he is making and the strategies he is employing. The children also offer their texts for public scrutiny.

Through this explicit joint exploration of narrative texts, Peter is encouraging the children to make discoveries, connections and generalisations about how successful Narratives work, so that they can then transfer these insights to their own writing. They "read like writers", always on the lookout for clues to improve their own texts. They know that writers are forever making deliberate choices as they craft their stories – choices about the characters, incidents, atmosphere, and so on – in an attempt to enhance the development of the whole. They are also aware that the more they themselves know about stories, and the language of stories, the more options they have when creating stories of their own.

This informed knowledge about Narrative is evident not only in their own story writing. Their book reviews now go beyond a basic gut reaction to what they've read. They are able to summarise the major stages of the story concisely, drawing on their awareness of narrative structure, and to evaluate specific features of the text.

Unhappily Ever After   by Paul Jennings

This story is about a cruel hearted headmaster named Mr. Brown who likes to belt children, but he goes a bit overboard and ends up in hell for his unjust ways.

The story takes place at a boarding school. It starts with Albert Jenkins about to receive a belting for supposedly writing a little note that said "Bald Brown went to town riding on his pony". After the cruel belting Albert stands there as though he hadn't received the punishment. Brown, feeling infuriated, decides to go for a row at the local beach to calm himself down. When he is a few kilometres away from the shore, a turbulent current grips the boat and takes it into a water spiral which has grooves and every groove contains a vision of someone paying the consequence for being unjust. Brown thinks it is a dream but instead he is actually in hell with a towering Albert Jenkins who races over to the cupboard and grabs the belt.

What I like about Unhappily Ever After is the twist in the resolution which makes it have a false ending which then goes into the real ending. The false resolution makes it a bit hard to understand at first, but once you see what it means you realise that it is Brown's chance to become a nicer person and be saved from hell but he doesn't take his chance and remains obstinant. As the old saying goes "Treat people how you want to be treated" which is where Brown went wrong.

Nikolai

And in peer conferences they can now offer constructive suggestions to their classmates:

Kristy: What kind of story would you call it?
Corey: Narrative.
Ben: Where's it set at?
Corey: My brother and I went to Jamberoo Recreation Park.
Kristy: What's the complication?
Corey: When they jump off the rock.
Kristy: That's not really a complication, how they jump off the rock.
Ben: Maybe it's a Recount.
Kristy: Yeah, it's what he *did*.
Mr B: So do you want to write a Recount or make it into a Narrative?
Corey: A Narrative.
Mr B: So how could we make it into a Narrative?
Corey: Put in a problem.
Mr B: So what sort of problem could you have when you jump off the rock?
Corey: Break a leg.
Kristy: Gets stuck in the bottom?
Ben: Something grabs his leg!

Peter's role in these exploration sessions varies from minute to minute. At times he takes the initiative, introducing a text, guiding the discussion, and drawing the children's attention to certain aspects. At other times the children take on this role, raising questions about texts they are reading and exchanging observations, while Peter sits back and learns from them.

Summary of Text Features

NARRATIVES (Recounts with a twist)

Purpose

The basic purpose of Narratives is to entertain, i.e. to gain and hold the reader's interest in a story. But Narratives may also seek to teach or inform, to embody the writer's reflections on experience, and – perhaps most important – to nourish and extend the reader's imagination.

Types

There are many types of Narratives. They are typically imaginary but can be factual. They include fairy stories, mysteries, science fiction, choose-your-own-adventures, romances, horror stories, "heroes and villains" (e.g. TV cartoons), adventure stories, parables, fables and moral tales, myths and legends, historical narratives.

Text Organisation

The focus of the text is on a sequence of actions.

The Narrative usually begins with an **orientation,** where the writer attempts to sketch in or create the "possible world" of this particular story. The reader is introduced to the main character(s) and possibly some minor characters. Some indication is generally given of *where* the action is located and *when* it is taking place. An "atmosphere" is usually established and there is often some foreshadowing of the action to follow, drawing readers into the story and making them want to become involved. The orientation may be brief ("Mr Fox went out hunting one night"), or it may extend for several pages. The sort of details chosen for inclusion are those which will enhance the later development of the story (e.g. the personality of the main character(s), the type of situation, the relationship with other characters).

SAMPLE TEXT: NARRATIVE

Text Organisation

Language Features

who?

where?

orientation

John slumped in the beanbag, his arms crossed and his face with a gloomy frown. He was a new kid in town but no-one knew he was even there. John wasn't the type of person you could have fun with. He didn't like anybody and they didn't like him. All day he sat hunched in the beanbag staring blankly out the window.

variety of verbs/processes
· linking
· mental
· action/material

complication

Through the window he caught a glimpse of a gigantic hollow tree in a vacant lot. The tree seemed to beckon him. He stood slowly up as if he was in a trance, then started to walk towards the tree. Its branches were scraggly and tough, its roots dug into the ground like claws. The tree had thorns all over it and vines hung around it. John tried to turn away but he couldn't. A mysterious force was pulling him into the hollow.

linking words to do with time

specific participants

resolution

John never reappeared ... but no-one noticed or cared.

Steven (10)

The story is pushed along by a series of events, during which we usually expect some sort of **complication** or problem to arise. It just wouldn't be so interesting if something unexpected didn't happen. This complication will involve the main character(s) and often serves to (temporarily) thwart them from reaching their goal. Narratives mirror the complications we face in life and tend to reassure us that they are resolvable.

In a "satisfying" Narrative, a **resolution** of this complication is brought about. The complication may be resolved for better or for worse, but it is rarely left completely unresolved (although this is of course possible in certain types of Narrative which leave us wondering "How did it end?").

There may in fact be a major complication in the Narrative which is not resolved until the end, with a number of minor complications along the way, which might be resolved in part or whole as they arise or later in the story. These are usually related to the major complication and serve to sustain the interest and suspense, leading to a crisis or climax.

Language Features

- Specific, often individual participants with defined identities. Major participants are human, or sometimes animals with human characteristics.

- Mainly action verbs [*material processes*], but also many verbs which refer to what the human participants said, or felt, or thought [*verbal and mental processes*].

- Normally past tense.

- Many linking words to do with time.

- Dialogue often included, during which the tense may change to the present or future.

- Descriptive language chosen to enhance and develop the story by creating images in the reader's mind.

- Can be written in the first person (I, we) or third person (he, she, they). (In choose-your-own-adventures, the reader is involved in the story as a major character and addressed as "you".)

Language Highlight

DIFFERENT TYPES OF PROCESSES

One of the major functions of language is to enable us to represent the world – and not only the real world but imaginary, possible worlds. The world is made up of people, places, objects, animals, plants, concepts, machines and so on. But the world is not static – it also involves events and happenings. We could describe the world in terms of **processes** and **participants** in those processes. We could see a text as representing those participants and processes in language, e.g.

The children	were reading	their novels.
participant	*process*	*participant*

The processes represent "what's going on in the world". In traditional grammar, processes are referred to as "verbs". We may generally think of verbs as "doing" words. But this is rather vague, and not entirely accurate.

There are many types of processes going on in the world:

- the "doings": the actions and happenings we observe taking place around us (he walked, they drove, it rained), referred to as *material processes*

- the processes that humans engage in with their intellect and senses, referred to as *mental processes*, e.g.

  believing, knowing (*processes of cognition*)
  seeing, observing (*processes of perception*)
  fearing, enjoying (*processes of feeling/affect*)

- the "talking" or *verbal processes* (he said, she accused, they promised).

Each of these processes refers to a different type of reality:

- the reality of the "real world" (*material*)

- the reality as perceived and interpreted through the senses (*mental*)

- the reality we construct through language (*verbal*).

In Narratives, we create a particular "world". This world imitates the characteristics of the real world – things are happening, people are thinking and feeling, listening and talking. So, in a Narrative, we would expect to find a great variety of process types.

In other genres, however, there may be an emphasis on only one or two types of process. In a Recount or Instructions, for example, the emphasis is on actions and events, so material processes will predominate.

In texts which are more concerned with "things" rather than "actions", we often find a different type of process. In Reports and Descriptions, for example, we tend to find sentences like the following:

Echidnas *belong to* the group called monotremes – egglaying mammals.

They *are* small, yellow-brown, round-shaped creatures with long noses.

They *have* sharp claws for digging and spikes to protect them.

These are not "doing" words at all, and yet they include what are perhaps the most commonly used verbs in the English language. Their function is to form a link between bits of information. We could call them "linking" verbs or *relational processes* because they relate one part of the clause to another.

Echidnas *belong to* the group called monotremes – egglaying mammals.
(linking the subject to its larger group – classification)

They *are* small, yellow-brown, round-shaped creatures with long noses.
(linking the subject to its characteristics: size, colour, shape, etc.)

They *have* sharp claws for digging and spikes to protect them.
(linking the subject to its parts, components)

There is another common type of process which is not a "doing" verb. It simply indicates that something "exists":

There are many drought-stricken countries in the world today.

There exists an urgent need for famine relief.

There is no simple solution to the problem.

These are called *existential processes*.

SUMMARY OF PROCESS TYPES

doing/happening	*material*	
	mental	{ *cognition* *perception* *affect*
	verbal	
being/having	*relational* *existential*	

Finally, let's return to Narrative and look at the variety of processes employed in a short extract from E. Nesbit's *The Railway Children*, where the children and their mother are nearing the end of their journey to a new home in the country. Notice how the text is not a bare recital of events, but is constantly enriched by suggestions of what the characters perceive, think, feel and say.

material

They woke up, cold and melancholy, and stood shivering on the draughty platform while the baggage was taken out of the train. Then the engine, puffing and blowing, set to work again, and dragged the train away. The children watched the tail-lights of the guard's van disappear into the darkness.

material

material

This was the first train the children saw on that railway which was in time to become so very dear to them. They did not guess then how they would grow to love the railway, and how soon it would become the centre of their new life nor what wonders and changes it would bring to them. They only shivered and sneezed and hoped the walk to the new house would not be long. Peter's nose was colder than he ever remembered it to have been before. Roberta's hat was crooked, and the elastic seemed tighter than usual. Phyllis's shoe-laces had come undone.

relational *mental* *mental* *relational* *mental* *material* *mental* *relational*

"Come," said Mother, "we've got to walk. There aren't any cabs here."

The walk was dark and muddy. The children stumbled a little on the rough road, and once Phyllis absently fell into a puddle, and was picked up damp and

verbal *existential* *relational* *material*

existential   unhappy. There were no gas-lamps on the
road, and the road was uphill. The cart
went at a slow pace, and they followed   *material*
the gritty crunch of its wheels. As their
eyes got used to the darkness, they could
mental   see the mound of boxes swaying dimly in
front of them.

A long gate had to be opened for the
cart to pass through, and after that the
road seemed to go across fields – and now
it went downhill. Presently a great dark
lumpish thing showed over to the right.

existential   "There's the house," said Mother. "I   *verbal*
wonder why she's shut the shutters."

mental   *material*

5 : INFORMATION REPORTS

Curriculum Context

COMMUNICATIONS – THE TELEPHONE

Soft gasps of wonderment as Mr Murphy lifted the casing off the telephone, revealing its innermost secrets. The naked telephone was no longer the familiar household object but a technological marvel of unsuspected complexity. Soon groups of children were sprawled around the room, eagerly absorbed in dismantling the phones Mr Murphy had brought with him.

Third class were involved in a theme on Communications, and Rasheeda, the ESL teacher, had decided that it would be appropriate within such a theme for the children to write an Explanation describing how the telephone system works. She realised, however, that in order to write with any confidence, they would first need to build up their knowledge of the field. It would be difficult to write about the working of the system without knowing about its different parts and their jobs. So, as a preliminary activity, the class would write an Information Report outlining the components of the telephone.

Mr Murphy, the father of one of the boys, was a Telecom technician who had offered to share his experience with the class. While the children were excitedly engaged in taking the phones apart, they exploited his expertise by asking endless questions:

What makes the dial spring back?

Why is there a bump on the "5" button?

What's this bit for?

Mr Murphy in turn would draw their attention to a particular component and ask if they knew its name, its function and how it worked.

"And what's this piece here?"

"The mouthpiece," several children volunteered.

"And if we screw it off, we find a transmitter – what do you think the transmitter does?"

"It sends your voice along the line."

"That's right. It transmits your voice to the person on the other end. How do you think it does that?"

"By electricity?" asked Tony tentatively.

"Good. The transmitter changes voice energy into electrical energy."

Rasheeda, in the meantime, was sitting at the computer keyboard, with the monitor facing the class. As the class became familiar with each component, Rasheeda would ask them to summarise their understandings in note-form, which she typed directly into the computer, with the monitor displaying the text in large print.

When Mr Murphy left, the class set about writing an Information Report on what they had discovered about telephones. They had written several Information Reports in the past, so Rasheeda built on this previous experience. They talked once more about the purpose of Information Reports (to document, organise and store information) and contrasted this with the purpose of a Narrative.

The class then quickly revised the structure of an Information Report by looking at several factual "big books" – both commercial and class-made. Because by now they had a good grasp of the overall structure of an Information Report, Rasheeda decided to concentrate on how to write a general opening statement. They looked at how each of the model texts introduced its major topic and, with these models in mind, each child composed a possible introduction to the class Information Report on "Telephones". Rasheeda then wrote a selection of these on the board and the class chose the one they felt was most effective:

> The telephone is only one piece of the giant jigsaw puzzle of communications. Although it is only one piece, it is the most important of all.

The children decided, however, that they wanted to add to this by mentioning the different types of telephones and outlining what they would cover in the Report:

> There are many different kinds of telephones. The main two kinds are the push-button and the dial. We are going to look at the parts inside the dial telephone and their uses.

Then the class broke into small groups, each group writing a description of one component of the telephone and its function. As they wrote, they referred to many sources of information – their own background knowledge about telephones (as well as that of their peers and Rasheeda), their observations of the dismantled phones, the expertise of Mr Murphy, the notes which Rasheeda had scribed for them on the computer, and some Telecom booklets which Mr Murphy had left for them.

When they came together once more, Rasheeda pasted each group's description onto a large sheet of butcher's paper under the opening statement so that the class could see the first draft of their Report. As a group they then read through the Report, redrafting it whenever they felt something was not clear.

When they were satisfied with the text, Rasheeda typed it up for them while they drew illustrations and diagrams. Copies were made for each child in the class and a couple for Mr Murphy and Telecom. Here is a sample page.

THE BELL

The BELL tells us that someone is calling. The electric bell is very similar to the door bell. The sound can be adjusted by a wheel under the case. The tone of the bell can be high or low. There are different telephones with different bells and different tones.

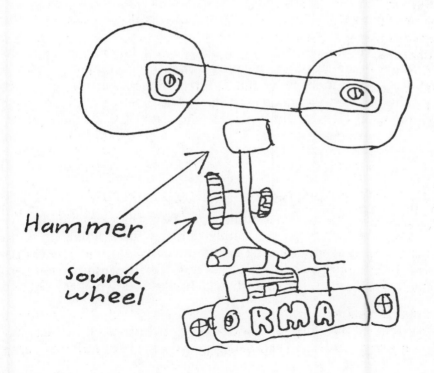

Focus Activity

MODELLING A REPORT

Rasheeda prefers to write her own model texts. This way she knows what is involved in the writing of a particular genre and can anticipate the sorts of difficulties the children might experience. She tries to keep the content of the text relatively simple so that they can concentrate on the structure and language features. She chooses a topic which is not the same as (though similar to) the one the children will be writing about. In a previous unit, for instance, when the class was studying Spiders, she had modelled a text on Redbacks and the children had chosen to write on Funnelwebs, Huntsmen or Trapdoors. So they were able to observe how such a text would be shaped, without being tempted to copy word for word from the model.

Once the children are familiar with the features of the genre, they move on from Rasheeda's rather basic models to commercially produced texts. Many of these are written by experts for other experts and so the language and structure are often too complex to use with children, but with increasing numbers of high-quality factual texts for children being published, the job of finding models is becoming much easier.

When modelling a text, Rasheeda usually starts by reading it to the children and then drawing their attention to its overall structure so that they can see "the big picture". After identifying the different stages that the text goes through, they discuss the function of each stage. The function of the opening stage of an Information Report, for example, is to state clearly what is being looked at and to make some general statement which usually locates it in the scheme of things, e.g.

> The Redback is one of the most dangerous spiders in Australia.

The function of the rest of the Report is to provide more detailed information about the topic. This information needs to be readily available to the reader, so it must be organised coherently. During the Spiders unit the children in Rasheeda's class had examined a number of Information Reports to find out how they approached their topics and how the information was organised. To help them do this, Rasheeda had asked what the Spider Report was telling us about in general, i.e.

> different types of poisonous spiders

and then what each paragraph/section was about, e.g.

one particular type of poisonous spider
- what it looks like
- where it is found
- what it eats
- unusual behaviour, etc.

The children then used different coloured highlighter pens to identify on their own copies the parts of the text which talked about appearance, location, behaviour, etc. This analysis helped to make explicit the sorts of details normally included in such texts and how they can be expressed, and it proved to be very useful when the children were later writing their own Information Reports. It enabled them to formulate similar focus questions to guide their research and the organising of their texts, e.g.

What do Huntsmen spiders look like?

Is the male different from the female?

Where do they live?

What do they eat?

In later modelling sessions Rasheeda demonstrated other language features, such as the use of examples. After whiting out all the examples from a text, she made an overhead transparency and asked the class to supply examples in the blank spaces. They then discussed how the use of examples helped to make the text easier to understand.

Summary of Text Features

INFORMATION REPORTS
(What an entire class of things is like)

Purpose

The function of an Information Report is to document, organise and store factual information on a topic. Information Reports classify and describe the phenomena of our world. We use them when we talk about a whole class of things, e.g."Bikes". By contrast, a Description only talks about one specific thing, e.g. "My Bike". Information Reports are written about living things like plants and animals, and non-living things like phones, bikes or oceans.

Types

The term "report" is used in everyday language to refer to many different types of factual texts – news reports, science reports, weather reports, etc. In this book, however, the term Information Report is being used in a very specific way to refer *only to texts used to store information about a class of things*. To use the term in this restricted way might at first prove a bit confusing when we are used to using it in a very broad way to refer to virtually any factual text. But unfortunately there is no readily available word in English for this type of text, and so, until one is coined, we'll have to use an expression like Information Report.

Information Reports can contain information of various kinds, e.g.

classification into different types (subclasses)
Are there different kinds of energy?
What are the different types of clouds?
What is the difference between frogs and toads?
How are plant cells different from animal cells?

an examination of **components**
What is the earth made of?
What are the parts of a compound microscope?
What do fireworks consist of?

a look at various **aspects**
How big is the universe? (size)
What is a gyroscope used for? (function)
What do bears do in winter? (behaviour)
How is parliament organised? (system)

Text Organisation

The major focus is on a "thing" (or, more accurately, a class of things) rather than a sequence.

The topic of the Report is usually introduced by an
opening general statement/general classification
locating what is being talked about in the universe of things. It often takes the form of a classification or definition (e.g. Bikes are a popular form of transport). Sometimes the opening statement may also indicate a particular aspect of the topic that is being treated (e.g. There are many different types of bike in Australia).

The rest of the Report will consist of
facts about various aspects of the subject.

These facts will be grouped into topic areas, each marked by a topic sentence to indicate the particular aspect of the subject being dealt with. Each aspect might be elaborated by referring to distinctive characteristics of the subject (colour, shape, habits, behaviour, etc.), or by giving examples, or by comparing and contrasting, or by describing components and their function.

Reports don't usually contain an "ending", although sometimes the detailed information is rounded off by some general statement about the topic (e.g. Stamps can provide hours of enjoyment for young and old).

Paragraphing should help to organise the information effectively. Sub-headings or other graphic devices may be used to introduce different areas of the topic.

Diagrams, photos and illustrations are often used to lend clarity to the text and may be accompanied by labels or captions. The captions usually link the graphic to the text.

Language Features

- Generalised participants: a whole class of things (e.g. volcanoes, news-papers, the royal family) rather than specific participants (e.g. Mt Vesuvius, *The Times*, Queen Elizabeth).

- Some action verbs *[material processes]*, especially when describing behaviour (climb, eat, erupt).

- Many "linking" verbs *[relational processes]* (is, are, has, have, belongs to); see **Language Highlight**, p. 44.

- Usually in the "timeless" present tense (are, exist, grow).

- Descriptive language, but factual and precise rather than imaginative or "lively"; e.g. to convey
    what they look like (colour, shape, size, etc.)
    what they have (body parts, components, etc.)
    what they do (habits, behaviour, functions, uses, etc.).

- Language for defining, classifying, comparing and constrasting (are called, belong to, can be classified as, are similar to, are more powerful than).

- Likely to contain technical vocabulary.

- The writing is in a relatively formal and objective style. The use of first person pronouns (I, we) and the writer's opinions are not generally appropriate in this type of writing.

SAMPLE TEXT: INFORMATION REPORT

Text Organisation		Language Features

Text Organisation

general classification

description

Language Features

technical terms

Snakes are reptiles (cold-blooded creatures). They belong to the same group as lizards (the scaled group, Squamata) but form a sub-group of their own (Serpentes).

"timeless" present tense

linking verbs

<u>Appearance</u>
Snakes have no legs but a long time ago they had claws to help them slither along.

Snakes are not slimy. They are covered in scales which are just bumps on the skin. Their skin is hard and glossy to reduce friction as the snake slithers along the ground.

generalised participants

moderating words

<u>Behaviour</u>
Snakes often sunbake on rocks in the warm weather. This is because snakes are cold-blooded and they need the sun's warmth to heat their body up.

Most snakes live in the country. Some types of snakes live in trees, some live in water, but most live on the ground in deserted rabbit burrows, in thick, long grass and in old logs.

A snake's diet usually consists of frogs, lizards and mice and other snakes. The Anaconda can eat small crocodiles and even wild boars.

action verbs

Many snakes protect themselves with their fangs. Boa Constrictors can give you a bear hug which is so powerful it can crush every single bone in your body. Some snakes are protected by scaring their enemies away like the Cobra. The Flying Snake glides away from danger. Their ribs spread apart and the skin stretches out. Its technique is just like the sugar glider's.

comparison

John, Stefan & Joseph (year 5)

Language Highlight

DIFFERENT WAYS OF KNOWING

The participants in a young child's world are specific and everyday – Mum and Dad, the family dog, the mulberry tree in the backyard, the swingset, Aunt Cathy. It is a world of known individuals, familiar objects, specific incidents. It's an important world where the child comes to about know the self and relationships with others. It's a world where feelings are explored, opinions expressed, attitudes developed. It's the sort of world embodied in texts such as casual conversations, Morning News, Recounts and Narratives. Let's look at the language features of such texts:

specific time

specific incidents

personal pronouns

specific participants/ known individuals

opinions/feelings

Yesterday Aunt Cathy came to visit us. She played with Benji and me in the backyard. First of all I had a go on the swingset, then I climbed the mulberry tree and tore my jeans. Mum was real mad.

But when a child goes to school there are other worlds to explore. One of the functions of school in our culture is to take the child beyond the personal, commonsense world of particular instances and into new worlds of **generalised** phenomena – plants, animals, societies, land masses, mathematical operations, historical eras, weather patterns. The child's random knowledge becomes organised into discrete disciplines such as biology, history, chemistry, geography and maths. The child becomes an apprentice biologist, an apprentice historian, an apprentice chemist – inducted into the various ways of knowing about the world. The apprentice makes hypotheses, collects and analyses data, compares and contrasts, generalises, classifies and draws conclusions. The child's learning is formalised and systematised into the different ways of knowing valued in our society and necessary for full participation in it.

This generalised, systematised knowledge is reflected in the language features characteristic of such texts as Reports, Explanations, Instructions, and Arguments.

What is an alloy?

generalised participants

Alloys are mixtures of two or more pure metals. When pure metals are mixed to make an alloy, their properties change.

technical terms

The pure metal iron, for example, turns rusty when exposed to oxygen. When it is mixed with other pure metals such as chromium and nickel, it forms the alloy stainless steel. One of the properties of stainless steel is its resistance to rust.

generalised processes / "timeless" present tense

In this text we find a generalised knowledge embodied in such participants as "alloys", "pure metals", "properties". The tense also indicates that we are not concerned with specific incidents located at a particular point in time, but rather with "timeless" processes of an enduring nature (e.g. "are", "change", "turns"). Because the text is not about personal feelings and attitudes, the language is objective. It also includes a number of technical terms. The aim of such texts is to be as clear and precise as possible, rather than lively and colourful, and members of a discipline use technical terms to refer concisely and unambiguously to some phenomenon. Accordingly children who are being inducted into a discipline need to become familiar with the specialised language of that discipline.

An awareness of the different ways of knowing and the texts associated with them has implications for the teacher, particularly in programming. It helps to clarify the purpose of a unit of work through identifying not only the major understandings to be developed but also which types of texts the children might read and write in order to develop these understandings.

Let us say, for instance, that the aim of a particular unit is to develop an understanding of classification, and that the teacher has chosen trees as a case study. The ultimate product from such a unit might well be a Report written by the children on different types of trees. This could be preceded by activities to familiarise the children with the concept of classifying, such as collecting the leaves of various trees and grouping them according to certain characteristics (shape, colour, length, texture, etc.), looking at the characteristics botanists use when classifying different trees, coming to an understanding of certain technical terms employed in this field, researching the field from reference books, or examining model Information Reports which deal with classification. It would not further the aims of this unit to immerse the children in texts embodying specific knowledge by having them learn "Ode to a Tree", sing "The Old Oak Tree", write about "A Day in the Life of a Tree", or read "My Favourite Tree". We don't need to patronise children by assuming they cannot cope with the generalised knowledge and language of science. Children in fact are usually eager to investigate the world and, depending on the expectations of the teacher, take their role of apprentice quite seriously.

6 : EXPLANATIONS

Curriculum Context

HOW DOES THE TELEPHONE SYSTEM WORK?

Rasheeda's class were quite proud of themselves. They could talk knowledgeably about the different parts of the telephone and had produced an impressive Report. Now they were keen to find out how the whole system worked.

Mr Murphy came back the next day, this time loaded up with cables and switches. Once more the room buzzed with activity as the children passed cables around, unravelled them, examined the various colour-coded strands, and compared the old paper-wrapped wires with the more modern plastic-coated ones. Mr Murphy showed them how the small cable from the house grows and grows as it joins with others from the street and the neighbourhood on its way to the "pits" and "pillars", through the underground tunnels and finally to the exchange.

Again the questions kept flying as the children tried to work out how all the components link up and function together. Oral language was being used to enquire, to answer questions, to offer information, to explain to peers, to tell peers to do things, to exclaim.

With the help of posters and booklets, Mr Murphy described how a phone call is made, from the moment we pick up the handset through to when the call is received at the other end. As before, Rasheeda sat at the computer, typing up the children's oral summaries of how each part of the system works.

By now the children appeared to be fairly comfortable with the field – the different parts of the system, the technical terms naming those parts, how each part works and the function it has in the overall system, and how all these parts operate together. But just to clarify any lingering misunderstandings, Mr Murphy took them all to the local exchange, pointing out the pits and pillars along the way.

Now they were ready to write their Explanation. The class hadn't written an Explanation before, so Rasheeda supplied them with a couple of model texts from the Telecom booklets explaining how the telephone system works. They discussed the purpose of such a text and decided that it is a bit like a Report because it gives information, but that it doesn't only describe something, it also tells you how it works.

Before they wrote their own texts, Rasheeda felt that it would help if they first composed an Explanation as a whole class.

Focus Activity

JOINT CONSTRUCTION

In small groups the children brainstormed what they felt would need to be included in an Explanation of how the phone system works. Then Rasheeda brought the whole class together on the floor and sat herself in the middle at the overhead projector. Together they constructed a flowchart outlining the phone system. They would refer to this as they composed their Explanation.

The children then volunteered some opening statements which Rasheeda wrote on the transparency:

"We need two wires coming from the house to the road ..."

"First you have to dial the phone number ..."

"When you make a phone call it goes to the exchange ...."

With Rasheeda's guidance, they eventually decided on an opening statement which gave a more general introduction to the system:

The telephone system is made up of many different parts which all work together to help us make a phone call.

Once they had got started on the text there was no stopping them. By now quite familiar with the subject-matter, they confidently contributed to the growing text.

But they were not only concerned with getting the facts down. Much of the discussion centred on what details to include and how they should actually structure the text:

"Wouldn't it be better to talk about the caller first?"

"I reckon we should put in the bit about STD calls."

"No, that makes it too complicated. Just normal phone calls."

At times there were also lively debates about language features:

"We should put 'cables', not 'wires'."
"It's the same thing."
"No it's not. Cables are lots of wires joined together."

"We keep repeating 'the exchange', 'the exchange', 'the exchange'."
"Let's put 'it' instead."
"But they won't know what 'it' is!"
"Yes they will 'cause we've already said it."

Even spelling and punctuation did not go unnoticed:

"Mrs Flight, you've spelt 'receiver' wrong."
"Have I, David? How would you spell it?"

Rasheeda meanwhile warmly accepted their offerings. But her role was not simply that of a passive scribe. With her adult knowledge of how a text works, she was in a position to guide them towards a clearer, more coherent Explanation:

"Here you've said, 'The caller *dials* the number ...' but down here you've said, 'The person on the other end *picked* up the phone ...'. Do you think it would be better to say 'picked' or 'picks'?" ... "Why?"

"This bit sounds like how we would say it when we're *speaking*, but when we're *writing* we might say it differently. Who can suggest a more 'written' way of saying that?"

"How could we link up these two sentences?"

"I think we might need to put in a bit more detail about what happens at the exchange. It's a bit hard to understand."

"Do you think we need a new paragraph here?"

Joint construction provided an environment where the children actively participated in the creation of a text, where their contributions were valued, where they shared their knowledge about the topic and about language, and where the teacher was able, within context, to explicitly discuss with them those aspects of language which helped the text to fulfil its purpose more effectively.

Following the joint construction, the children went off the write their own Explanations.

HOW THE PHONE SYSTEM WORKS

The four-wire cable that comes from the telephone goes to a little concrete pit.
The four-wire cable becomes a four-pair cable and goes from the concrete pit to

an above-ground telephone pillar. From the pillar the wire becomes a ten-pair cable which goes from the pillar to underground tunnels. The ten-pair cable becomes a fifty-pair cable. The tunnels go under roads all around the city to other people's phones. The underground tunnels also go to the telephone exchange. From the telephone exchange, overseas phone calls go to Sydney international telephone exchange and then on to a satellite such as OTC. Overseas phone calls also go through submarine cables set deeply into the seabed. Normal calls go through the fifty-pair cable through the tunnels then a ten-pair cable to the telephone pillar then a four-pair cable to the concrete pit then a two-pair cable to your friend's home.

Daniela (first draft)

Summary of Text Features

EXPLANATIONS (Why is it so?/How does it work?)

Purpose
To give an account of how something works or reasons for some phenomenon.

Types
There is still much research to be done in identifying and describing different genres. The Explanation genre has not yet been studied in great detail, but commonsense might suggest at least two basic types of Explanation:

A) explaining *how*, e.g.

   Mechanical explanation (How does a pump work?)
   Technological explanation (How does a computer work?)
   System explanation (How does a company work?)
   Natural explanation (How are mountains formed?)

B) explaining *why*, e.g.

   Why do some things float and others sink?
   Why is the ozone layer thinning?
   Why do we have different seasons?
   Why does iron go rusty?
   Why do living things need food?

SAMPLE TEXT: EXPLANATION

**Text
Organisation**

**Language
Features**

How are sedimentary rocks formed?

phenomenon Sedimentary rock is formed by the
compression of layers of particles into a   *generalised*
solid form. Sediments such as sand and   *non-human*
explanation mud settle onto the floors of oceans and   *participants*
lakes. Over a long period of time, several
layers of sediments collect on the floor.   *action verbs/*
These layers are pressed together for many   *"timeless"*
thousands of years, fusing the small solid   *present tense*
particles of mud and sand to form solid
rock. This type of rock is called   *some*
sedimentary rock.   *passives*

Text Organisation

Explanations have a "process" focus rather than a "thing" focus. They are often concerned with a logical sequence.

To position the reader, there is usually some
statement about the phenomenon in question
(often in the form of a heading or question), followed by a
(sequenced) explanation of how/why something occurs.

Language Features

• Generalised non-human participants (the wind, glaciers, computers).

• Time relationships (first, then, following, finally), especially in type A.

• Cause-and-effect relationships (if/then, so, as a consequence, since), especially in type B.

• Mainly action verbs *[material processes]* (falls, rises, changes).

• Some passives (is saturated, are changed).

• Timeless present tense (are, happens, turns).

Language Highlight

MORE FEATURES OF WRITTEN TEXTS (Packing it in)

Spoken language slips away the moment it is uttered. If we want to understand what is being said, our listening has to keep up with the speaker. Writing, however, captures thoughts, transforming them into permanent texts that can then be read at our leisure. With written language we can take our time and re-read bits we haven't comprehended on our first reading. Written texts exploit this advantage by trying to pack more meanings into each clause. Let's have a look at some of the ways in which they do this by examining a typical written text (the main clauses have been numbered).

Hubble's Theory

1. Hubble's finding about the expansion of the galaxies revolutionised our understanding of the Universe and its origins.

2. If galaxies are flying apart,

3. then once upon a time they must all have been packed closely together.

4. This assumption led to the theory that the entire Universe once formed an infinitely dense, infinitely hot ball comprising all space and matter that for some unknown reason exploded.

5. That explosion is called the Big Bang,

6. and it marks the origin of the Universe as we know it.

7. There is no sign that the expansion of the Universe is slowing to a halt.

Lexical Density

By looking at the number of content words (**lexical** items – nouns, verbs, adjectives, etc.) we can see how many meanings have been packed into the one clause. Look at clause 4, for example: assumption; led; theory; entire Universe; formed; infinitely dense, infinitely hot ball; space; matter; unknown reason; exploded. That's a lot to come to terms with in the space of a few lines. Imagine if we *spoke* like that and you had to process all those meanings before the next sentence. That's one reason why it is so hard to take in a lecture or speech which is being read from a written text. A written text makes no concessions to the listener.

Let's compare the above text with the following text spoken by a child who had been asked how the Universe was formed.

1. "Well maybe there was this big planet

2. and it got too hot inside

3. and exploded into little pieces

4. and then the little pieces went closer to some planets

5. because the planets had gravity

6. and what happened was space sucked out all the gravity

7. before the pieces could reach the planets

8. so they just stopped where they were

9. and kept circling around the planets."

We can see from this text that in spoken language we tend not to introduce too many new meanings at once – perhaps only a couple per clause – letting the listener keep up with us.

The written text is "all compacted up", as the child described it. Linguists would say that it is "lexically dense", with sentences consisting of only one or two clauses, but those clauses are each packed with meanings. The spoken text on the other hand is a single "sentence" consisting of a long string of clauses, each containing only a couple of meanings (many of which are repeated during the text).

Nominalisation

A favourite ploy of adult writers is to take a "process" and turn it into a "thing". Have a look at the first sentence of the written text. If we were speaking that sentence, we would probably say something like:

> "There was this man called Hubble and he discovered that the galaxies keep expanding into space. Because of what he discovered, we now understand the Universe and how it began quite differently."

Look at what happened when we "unpacked" the written text:

NOUN/THING		VERB/PROCESS
Hubble's *finding*	became	he *discovered*
the *expansion*	became	*keep expanding*
our *understanding*	became	we *understand*
its *origins*	became	how it *began*

A term to describe what we do when we express a process as a "thing" or participant is **nominalisation.** Adult writers commonly use nominalisation to pack more meanings into the clause. You can only have one verb in a clause, but you can have several nouns. In the first sentence of the written text, for example, there is only one verb ("revolutionised") but there are several processes expressed as nouns ("finding", "expansion", "understanding", "origins").

Another reason for using nominalisation is to help us structure a text. We often explain something that happens by using verbs. But then we want to move the argument along, so we use a noun to condense what we have just described into a "thing" or concept. Look again at the written text to see how the writer has done this:

> The hypothesis that "If galaxies are flying apart, then once upon a time they must all have been packed closely together" is immediately summarised by "This assumption ...".

> The notion that "the entire Universe once formed an infinitely dense, infinitely hot ball comprising all space and matter that for some unknown reason exploded" can similarly be referred to as "That explosion ...".

> Once the process whereby the Universe is constantly expanding has been explained, it can be encapsulated in the noun group "the expansion of the Universe".

The Noun Group *[Nominal Group]*

Another reason why writers may prefer to use nouns is that you can keep building up meanings around nouns, turning them into lengthy structures and thereby compressing even more meanings into the clause.

Look at some of the noun *[nominal]* groups in the written text (the "head" noun is printed in italic type).

> Hubble's *finding* about the expansion of the galaxies
>
> our *understanding* of the Universe and its origins
>
> an infinitely dense, infinitely hot *ball* comprising all space and matter

The last example shows most clearly how the nominal group can call on a variety of resources, each providing further information about the thing in question. It's unusual to find such lengthy groups in spoken conversation.

Another Example

Let's now look at a text from the unit described in the next chapter. The class had been brainstorming ideas for a joint construction about shoplifting. Eventually the teacher identified the main points which were coming out of the discussion and asked one of the children to pull them together – the first step in moving into the more synoptic written mode.

CHILD'S SPOKEN VERSION

1. "Um ... ah ... whenever people steal things ... ah ...
2. you go to ...
3. just say somebody steals something from K-Mart
4. and they find out
5. but they didn't catch you
6. and they increase all the prices
7. because if they steal something two or three hundred dollars
8. you have to pay for that
9. 'cause the prices increase."

As a demonstration of moving from oral language to written, the teacher provided a "scaffold" by extracting three major points from this oral text and writing them in note form on the board. He then asked the children to develop them into a written text, with this result:

CHILDREN'S WRITTEN VERSION

1. Every day shops lose thousands of dollars worth of valuable items.

2. This affects us all

3. because prices increase

4. and we have to pay extra.

If an adult were to transform these ideas into writing, the sentence might look like this:

ADULT'S WRITTEN VERSION

The daily loss of thousands of dollars worth of valuable stock ultimately affects us all through an increase in prices.

Again it is obvious that writing is not simply "speech written down". The child's first attempt to summarise the discussion orally in preparation for writing was a string of clauses intricately linked by conjunctions such as "and", "but" and "because". Each clause contains only one or two main meanings, so the text is not lexically dense. The participants ("things") are expressed mainly by single words, so we don't have long nominal groups. And there is no nominalisation.

In the children's written version, however, irrelevancies have been eliminated and meanings compressed, leaving us with only four clauses. There is one long nominal group ("thousands of dollars worth of valuable items"); however, the text is still not very dense and there is no nominalisation.

The adult text condenses the meanings into one clause, resulting in a high level of lexical density (though this density has perhaps been achieved at some cost in clarity and vigour). The clause contains two nominal groups ("The daily loss of thousands of dollars worth of valuable stock" and "an increase in prices") and verbs have been converted to nouns ("loss", "an increase"). In addition, the notion of cause and effect, usually expressed by a conjunction (such as "because" in the children's text), has here been expressed by a preposition ("through").

The implications of all of this for the classroom are not clear-cut, but the following points might be worth considering.

§ When children are immersed in spoken language and written texts which are relatively close to spoken language (such as most Narratives and simplified factual texts), the transition to the sort of adult written texts marked by density, nominalisation and lengthy nominal groups may not always be as straightforward as we sometimes assume. This might help explain why older children often appear to have difficulties understanding their secondary textbooks. While all children need exposure to a wide range of genres, older children in particular need to engage with well-written texts which provide demonstrations of the features of compactly structured writing.

§ Children who develop an appreciation of the characteristics of such written texts are more likely to write in ways that may be expected of them as they grow older. Children who do not develop this appreciation may find that their texts are judged as immature.

§ Features such as the compact sentence, the clustering of meanings in nominal groups, and the use of nominalisation are some of the resources that mature writers draw upon when structuring written texts (particularly Reports, Explanations and Arguments). Like all resources they can be used effectively or badly. Our aim would not be to have children churning out lexically dense, highly nominalised texts as an end in itself, but rather to help develop an awareness, particularly in older children, of what resources are available to the writer and when it might be profitable to use them in order to construct coherent, concise texts. If such features are imposed as an orthodoxy, students might end up not only writing poor texts, but becoming alienated from writing altogether, perceiving it as boring and difficult.

§ Such understandings about written language are best developed in context and at the point of need – for example, while conferencing about a text which might benefit from some restructuring.

§ And of course, when evaluating students' writing, we can now recognise when a student is "stretching", approximating certain features of mature written texts, and offer encouragement and explicit assistance.

7 : ARGUMENTS

Curriculum Context

NED KELLY – GUILTY OR INNOCENT?

Mick was feeling uneasy about the narrow range of texts his class were producing. After all, these children would soon be in secondary school, where they would be expected to write in a number of factual genres. Their rambling fantasy thrillers and reworkings of last night's TV show would not be highly valued.

Mick decided to introduce the class to writing Arguments. He had been planning a history unit on Ned Kelly and by chance had come across a computer program which invited its users to become historians – to examine a database of original documents and transcripts relating to the trial and from the evidence to decide whether Kelly was guilty or innocent. This, Mick perceived, would provide a fertile context for the writing of Arguments.

Over the next couple of weeks the class became absorbed in the exploits of Kelly and his gang. Mick concentrated initially on developing their knowledge of the subject (or "field") so that they could draw on this when the time came to write. They brainstormed everything they knew about Ned Kelly. They read stories about his life and times. They watched Mick Jagger's interpretation of the Kelly legend on video. And they were constantly at the computer demanding information on the various incidents involving the Kelly gang, calling up witnesses, accessing documents and letters, and analysing transcripts of the court proceedings.

Mick encouraged the children to take responsibility for their own learning while they were developing their understanding of the field. One group in particular was eager to push ahead, so he decided to use them as a "seeding" group. They worked every spare minute on the project and became the class experts, available as peer tutors to help the other children find their way around the computer program.

While the children were busy familiarising themselves with the Kelly trial, Mick was also introducing them to the notion of logical argument. They had discussed the need to formulate an opinion and back it up with evidence, and they would earnestly scour the data, searching for clues of Kelly's guilt or innocence. Around the computer, and later in small groups, they would animatedly discuss their findings. They would bounce bits of evidence off each other, to be countered or confirmed.

They also discovered that some evidence contradicted previous evidence, and so, to highlight this, Mick surreptitiously arranged for two boys to start brawling in the middle of the class. He then asked the children for details of the fight – what had happened, who was involved, who started it, and so on. Many different versions were given, depending on the children's loyalties and perceptions. The next day Mick asked them to retell their observations and again their stories changed, demonstrating the unreliability of human memory – another factor in the Kelly trial.

The children by now were getting into some fairly weighty questions .... What is "truth"? What counts as evidence? Is a transcript more credible than a newspaper account? And they were becoming aware of the sort of language used in discussing such issues:

"You can't just say 'Ned Kelly was guilty', you've got to say 'I think ...' or 'In my opinion ...'."

"Or you could say 'maybe'."

"And then you've got to say 'because ...'."

"And we don't know for sure what Ellen Kelly did, so we have to say 'She said ...'."

Out of all this oral give-and-take, some tentative positions started to emerge. At this stage, Mick felt that they might benefit from some demonstrations of how to shape up relatively random ideas into a coherent Argument. So, since the children had made reference to the conflicting evidence in the Lindy Chamberlain trial, he wrote a model text arguing her case. As an experienced, literate adult, he had greater expertise in this genre and initially assumed more responsibility. Through some rather pointed questioning, he guided the children to the following discoveries about the function of the different stages of an Argument.

THE TRIAL OF LINDY CHAMBERLAIN

thesis statement (position)

In 1982 Lindy Chamberlain was convicted of murdering her baby Azaria while camping at Ayer's Rock. In my opinion, Lindy should not have been convicted for Azaria's murder as there is too much conflicting evidence.

argument · point A

(Firstly) there is the question of the blood found in the car. It was claimed that it was baby's blood. However, the tests used to identify the blood were later found to be unreliable and the blood could have come from an adult.

· point B

(Another) piece of conflicting evidence concerns the dingo. Lindy claimed that Azaria was taken by a stray dingo. Some of the other campers said that they saw no dingo, but there were several who confirmed Lindy's story, and who stated that they heard a dingo's cry just before Azaria went missing.

· point C

(And finally) there is the matter of the baby's jumpsuit which was later found with holes in it. The prosecution maintained that these holes could only have been made by a pair of nail scissors – the ones they claimed Lindy used to kill her baby. The defence on the other hand demonstrated that the holes could just as easily have been made by a dingo's teeth.

restatement of position

In the light of such conflicting evidence, I believe that it was wrong to convict Lindy Chamberlain without finding more definite proof of her guilt.

Mick then created opportunities for the children to have a go at jointly writing simple Arguments with familiar subject-matter. The classroom had been broken into during the week and the computer disks stolen. So as a class they composed a letter to the principal, urging the need for greater security and giving arguments to support their position. Later in the week, following an outbreak of shoplifting, Mick asked the children to decide whether the local shops should be lenient or hard on first-offenders. This time they wanted to put both sides of the argument before stating a position, and so, after an informal debate, they jointly constructed a slightly different type of expository text – a Discussion.

issue	Shopowners are losing a lot of money because of shoplifting. Should first offenders be let off lightly?
argument for	On the one hand, it's not fair to punish people the first time they make a mistake. The police should talk sternly to them and give them a warning.
argument against	On the other hand, every day shops lose thousands of dollars worth of valuable items. This affects us all because prices increase and we have to pay extra. So shopowners should come down heavy the first time to set an example.
conclusion	In our opinion, first offenders should be taught a lesson but the punishment might depend on questions such as how old they are, why they stole the goods, and so on.

This attempt at a Discussion was not entirely successful as the conclusion didn't draw upon the preceding arguments, but it was a satisfying approximation of the genre and the class felt a great sense of accomplishment.

As yet another demonstration of expository writing, Mick took the Ned Kelly drafts written by the "seeding" group, who had raced ahead of the rest, and made overhead transparencies of them. In the class conference which followed, the children suggested more effective ways of organising the various arguments.

The class now had a variety of model texts to refer to and had attempted the joint writing of expository texts with the assistance of Mick and their classmates. It was time to review what they knew about the Kelly trial, formulate their positions and argue their cases individually in writing.

The unit culminated in a re-enactment of the trial, with the children taking the roles of prosecutor, defence counsel, jury, judge, witnesses, and of course the accused – who was found guilty but, because of extenuating circumstances, was not hanged.

Focus Activity

CONFERENCING AND EVALUATION

Mick vividly remembers the frustration he used to feel when conferencing with the children during process writing. The abundant mistakes in spelling and punctuation were easily attended to while editing the drafts. But surely there was more he could do than simply correct errors and utter vague, encouraging comments. How could he give them specific suggestions to help improve their texts?

Having developed an understanding of how different texts work, Mick feels that his conferencing sessions are now much more productive. He can contribute in a positive way – helping the child to identify the purpose of the text being written and build on those aspects which help achieve this purpose.

His emphasis in conferencing is now on the development of an *effective* text and he is able to give constructive advice on how to go about it. He realises that different texts achieve their purposes in different ways, and that any appraisal of a text needs to take into consideration how success-fully it achieves its particular aim.

As an example, let's look at an early draft of part of Nicky's text.

The Stringybark Creek Incident

Ned was not guilty of a cold-blooded murder but he is still guilty for the shooting of Constables Scanlon and Kennedy, although he is not guilty of shooting Lonigan as it was in self defence.

Ned came across the shingle hut where the constables were staying Constables McIntyre and Lonigan were out the front of the hut. Ned had the option of shooting them without saying a word but not wishing to take a life Ned waited. Then after waiting a while they came out of the bushes and told them to bail up. McIntyre obeyed and put up his hands but Lonigan ran behind a stack of wood and took aim at the Kelly gang when Ned shot Lonigan in the right eye which was a fatal shot.

But McIntyre said that Lonigan didn't have time to run behind the woodstack and he was shot standing right next to him. He also says that Kennedy dis-mounted his horse and was shot and Scanlon was shot in the back as he turned to gallop away. McIntyre escaped on Kennedy's horse.

Mick's conferencing related back to previous modelling done in class:

"You've found some excellent information about the incident, Nicky. And you've made a judgement based on what you found out. Great, you're well on your way.

"At the beginning, I think we need to let the reader know a bit more about the incident and what Ned was being charged with, like you did in the Fitzpatrick Incident. The reader needs to know what the issue is.

"This is like a Discussion, isn't it? You're giving us Ned's version of what happened and then McIntyre's side, but it's not clear to the reader that this part is Ned's evidence and that this is Mcintyre's evidence. Maybe you need to state that at the beginning of each part.

"There's conflicting evidence there, so you've had to make up your mind, haven't you? You've stated your opinion at the beginning, which is fine, but it might be more appropriate in a Discussion to come up with your position after you've considered both pieces of evidence.

"You haven't mentioned what happened to Scanlon and Kennedy in Ned's evidence, so you'll need to give his story about them.

"By the way, who does 'they' refer to in 'they came out of the bushes'? Your reference needs to be more explicit for the reader."

Nicky had already produced quite a proficient expository text and Mick acknowledged its positive features – particularly the thorough research which had produced sufficient evidence to enable Nicky to draw a conclusion.

To enhance the effectiveness of the text, Mick pointed out that it needed to be more considerate of the reader by providing a context at the outset (stating the issue and any background information necessary), and by signalling the contradictory evidence later. He suggested rearranging parts of the text and adding missing evidence. Finally he commented on an ambiguous reference which might confuse the reader. Nicky's response to these suggestions led to considerable improvements in the final draft.

The Stringybark Creek Incident: What really happened?

Charge: Guilty of wilful murder of Constables Lonigan, Scanlon and Kennedy.

Ned's Evidence
Ned came across the shingle hut where the Constables McIntyre, Lonigan, Scanlon and Kennedy were staying. McIntyre and Lonigan were out the front of the hut. Ned stated that he had the option of shooting them without saying a word but not wishing to take a life Ned waited. Then after waiting a while, Ned's gang came out of the bushes and told them to bail up. McIntyre obeyed and put his hands up but Lonigan ran behind a stack of wood and took aim at the Kelly gang when Ned shot Lonigan in the right eye which was a fatal shot. Then constables Scanlon and Kennedy came back from patrolling. Kennedy slewed his horse around as if to gallop away but he took his revolver and fired, turned around again, loaded and then one of the Kelly gang shot him bringing him to the ground. Scanlon, dismounting from his horse, ran to the nearest tree and fired and ran to another tree further on and fired again and one of Ned's gang shot him under the arm which proved to be a fatal shot.

The Constables' Evidence
Constable McIntyre is the only one of the constables still alive to tell the story and he tells a very different story to Ned. He says that Lonigan didn't have time to run behind the woodstack and he was shot standing right next to him. He also

says that Kennedy dismounted his horse and was shot and Scanlon was shot in the back as he turned to gallop away.

My Conclusion
McIntyre's evidence is weak. He states that the bullets came from the back and not from the front. Dr. Nicholson finds the opposite, suggesting that Lonigan stood his ground and met Ned on equal terms. Kelly says that it was not murder but self defence and he gave Lonigan a chance to surrender. However, the fact is that Lonigan was doing his duty. Ned resisted arrest and shot him three times. The important thing is that Lonigan had power by law whilst Ned only had force of arms. Ned's argument has not succeeded as he was doing an illegal act at the time.

At this stage Mick's conferencing concentrated on the "meanings" being made in the text – the ideas, how they were organised and the way the text "hung together". Spelling, punctuation and other conventions could be treated during the editing phase.

During conferencing, Mick draws on the language concepts and terminology – the "language for talking about language" – which the class has built up in preceding sessions. He finds these shared understandings helpful when referring to various types of texts and their typical features. When commenting on the children's texts, Mick always attempts to explain the reason behind any suggestion, demonstrating how it might improve the text. In this way, the children are able to develop generalisations for future reference – an important step in becoming independent writers.

Because the class share explicit understandings about how texts work, they are able to identify criteria to help them when evaluating their own texts for revision and when conferencing with peers. Mick also uses these criteria when assessing the children's texts more formally for his records and for reporting on children's progress.

In the Ned Kelly unit, for example, Mick would make notes during each stage of the curriculum cycle about the children's developing proficiency in arguing a case, e.g.

- can understand the purpose of an Argument
- can distinguish between Argument and Discussion
- can recognise the different stages of the schematic structure of an Argument
- understands the function of each stage
- uses shared language terminology meaningfully
- can locate relevant information
- can formulate a position

- can back up assertions with evidence
- can detect contradictory evidence
- can actively participate in informal oral debate
- is aware of the reader's needs
- uses language to structure the argument
- organises arguments into appropriate paragraphs.*

In his assessment record, Mick now includes notes about the different types of genres the children attempt to use and their degree of success in controlling them. He makes specific references to what the children are able to do, and those aspects which they still need to work on, so that he is able to identify areas of need to help guide his programming.

---

* For more detailed suggestions regarding assessment, see **References** for publications by the DSP Literacy Project and M. Macken et al.

Summary of Text Features

ARGUMENT (Stating your case)

Purpose
To take a position on some issue and justify it.

Types
Argument texts belong to a genre group called "Exposition", concerned with the analysis, interpretation and evaluation of the world around us. There are several different expository genres, and choice depends on whether your major aim is to simply analyse, or to interpret, or to evaluate. Some texts contain a mixture of expository genres.

In an Argument the emphasis is on persuading someone to your point of view. You might be arguing simply to justify a position/interpretation ("persuading *that*"), or you might be arguing that some sort of action be taken ("persuading *to*"). Some examples are: convincing your parents to lend you the car; newspaper editorials; sermons; political speeches; certain essays; letters to the editor; debates.

Note

§ A "letter" is not a genre in itself but rather a medium for a number of different genres: e.g. a Recount of your trip abroad; a Report on the range of fax machines available; a Description of your new house; Directions as to how to open an account.

§ Debates in fact state and defend *two* opposing points of view. To distinguish this genre from Argument, we could call it "Discussion". It's commonly used in essays which require the writer to discuss both sides of a case and then form some opinion based on the preceding arguments. Even in writing an Argument it's useful to try to anticipate any opposing points of view in order to pre-empt any questions that might otherwise be raised in the reader's mind.

Text Organisation

The major focus is on an issue and a logical sequence of argument related to this issue.

The beginning of an Argument usually consists of a
statement of position *[thesis statement]*
often accompanied by some background information about the issue in question. There may also be some broad foreshadowing *[preview]* of the line of argument to follow.

To justify the position taken, the writer must now present the
argument.
Usually there is more than one *point* put forward in the argument, and each one should be supported by *evidence* (e.g. statistics, quotes), and possibly by examples. The points are carefully selected and developed to add weight to the argument. All points should relate directly back to the statement of position, and there are often internal links between the various points too.

At some stage the writer may suggest some resolution of the issue.

Finally, there is an attempt at
summing up the position
in the light of the argument presented, reaffirming the general issues under discussion and possibly calling for action.

Language Features

• Generalised participants – sometimes human but often abstract (issues, ideas, opinions, etc.) – unless the issue centres on a particular event or incident.

SAMPLE TEXTS: ARGUMENTS

Text Organisation		Language Features

Persuading to ...

Dear Sir,

issue On behalf of the residents of ,......., I would like to express our concern at the unreasonable amount of pollution created by the steel works in our area.

emotive words

argument The pollution is increasing and causing many problems for the neighbourhood.
* The sulphur fumes cause breathing difficulties when a north-easterly blows.
* The ash from the stack makes the washing dirty.
* The coal trucks are ruining the roads and making sleep impossible for shift-workers.

generalised participants

usually "timeless" present tense

recommendation We would like to suggest that an enquiry be held into the running of the steel mills and the impact on the local community.

some passives

variety of verbs/processes

We hope that you will give this matter serious consideration at your next meeting.

Yours sincerely,
Bruno Gallo

Persuading that ...

position I think it's good to be bald.
argument Firstly you don't have to wash your hair.
Secondly you don't have to comb your hair.
And thirdly you don't have to go to the barber.
summing up So you're lucky if you're bald.

connectives structuring the argument

logical connectives

Stef (7)

- Possibility of technical terms relating to the issue.

- Variety of verb *[process]* types – action *[material]*, linking *[relational]*, saying *[verbal]* and mental.

- Mainly timeless present tense when presenting position and points in the argument, but might change according to the stage of the text (e.g. if historical background to the issue is being given, the tense will obviously change to the past; if predictions are being made, the tense might change to the future).

- Frequent use of passives to help structure the text.

- Actions are often changed into "things" (nominalised) to make the argument sound more objective and to help structure the text (see p. 80).

- Connectives associated with reasoning (therefore, so, because of, the first reason, etc.).

- Arguments quite often employ emotive words (blatant disrespect, we strongly believe) and verbs such as "should". Such emotive language is more appropriate to spoken debate, and essays are generally more successful if the writer seeks to convince the reader through logic and evidence.

Language Highlight

THE POLITICS OF LANGUAGE (Tricks of the trade)

The language used in a written text is influenced by the audience for whom it is being written.

The writer of the editorial in an afternoon paper knows that his audience is probably made up of people who are skimming through the pages after work for relaxation. They are not interested in closely argued, academic debate. They want something relatively lightweight, perhaps something they can throw into a discussion over the dinner table or down at the pub. To get his point across, the editor appeals to the **emotions** by choosing value-laden words such as "bunkum", "tired old ploy", "political bigotry".

In a school context, however, the audience is often the teacher – the representative of a Western cultural tradition which puts a high value on analytical, logical thinking. There is an expectation that certain texts (often the more "prestigious" ones, which determine the degree of success or failure at school) will be written to appeal to the **intellect** rather than the emotions. Students' arguments need to be based on logic and defended with evidence, rather than openly expressing personal opinion arising out of intuition, feelings or prejudice. The language therefore will emphasise apparently objective rather than value-laden choices.

This expectation will of course depend on the age of the child and the genre in question. Young children are encouraged to express personal opinions freely – "I really love my cat"; "The excursion to the zoo was terrific". But as children mature and attempt to use language to get other people to share their point of view, they need to be able to justify their opinions.

In certain genres such as Recount, Narrative or Book Review, the open expression of opinion will always be regarded as quite appropriate. The purpose of these genres is to reflect on our personal world and explore our feelings, beliefs, relationships with others, etc. But in many "academic" genres such as Report, Explanation and Argument, the purpose is to analyse and examine the world in a rational way – to enter into a type of knowledge which goes beyond the self. These genres embody the "way of knowing" on which much of our Western technological society is built. (See **Language Highlight**, p. 55.)

In academic Arguments, then, the writer may be more persuasive when not intruding overtly into the text. Experienced writers become familiar with the resources of language which make it possible to "hide the self". Academics, journalists, lawyers and politicians in particular know how to manipulate language so as to appear impartial and objective.

Let us compare the text of a child on the issue of nuclear weapons with one from an adult.

CHILD'S TEXT

I am worried because one day the politicians might explode a nuclear bomb and everyone will die a horrible death.

ADULT TEXT

Concern has been expressed over the possible detonation of a nuclear device which could result in widespread mortality.

While the child's text is a forthright expression of anxiety, the adult writer's personality and point of view have been suppressed so far that the text could equally well belong to an Argument for or against retaining nuclear weapons. Let's look more closely at the language features used to achieve this effect.

i) The **personal pronoun** "I" has been removed. The adult author no longer speaks on behalf of himself or herself alone, but assumes a representative voice.

ii) Through nominalisation, **actions** (verbs) have become **things** (nouns):

ACTION   THING
I am worried   >   concern
might explode   >   the possible detonation
everyone will die   >   widespread mortality

If the actions disappear from the text, then so do those who perform them. No longer is there an identifiable, real *person* ("I") who is worried, no longer are *people* such as politicians exploding the bomb, no longer are there *people* dying.

This is a common ploy of adult writers when they don't want to be explicit about who is involved in or responsible for certain actions. (See p. 64 for other uses of nominalisation.)

iii) Similarly, the actors can be removed by using the **passive** voice (e.g. "Concern *has been expressed*" ... by whom?).

iv) **Abstract and technical terms** have replaced more emotive, everyday words: *worried* has become "concern"; *explode* has become "detonation"; *bomb* has become "device"; *death* has become "mortality". Personal opinion, as expressed by *horrible,* is no longer present – the text has been neutralised. The average person in the street tends to be excluded from the issue, which is now discussed clinically by the knowledgeable expert. The technical terminology lends a scientific aura to the text. The fallible human has been eliminated.

v) The adult writer, with a greater experience of the world, is more aware of the **differing degrees of certainty** with which we can make claims. To win an argument, children often exaggerate and make sweeping generalisations. An adult knows that the reader will become sceptical and the argument will be jeopardised if bald statements and unqualified claims are made. An adult leaves room for negotiation by using words such as "nearly", "often", "most", "generally", "tend to", "might", etc. In the adult text, notice how "could" has been used to avoid charges of overstating the case.

vi) Cause-and-effect is usually expressed through conjunctions like "because" and "therefore". However, in written texts particularly, cause-effect and other relations are also expressed by using nouns (The first *reason* ...) or, as here, verbs (could *result* in ...), or prepositions (*through* ...), to give more structural choices and often more subtle connections.

The language resources described above are not necessarily devious, though they can of course be employed to baffle or mislead. Proficient users of English draw on them constantly for a variety of straightforward purposes, and with growing maturity many children will learn to draw on them too. If we give children an explicit awareness of how these language features operate, they will be in a better position to become critical readers and listeners, and to shape language discriminatingly to their own ends.

POSTSCRIPT

TIPS FOR THE EXPLORER

When you start looking closely at texts (for example, when you are searching for models or conferencing with your students), you will find that not all texts have such a readily recognised schematic structure as those included in this book. The model texts discussed in these chapters have been selected because they display features typical of the genre they represent. When we are modelling texts it is a good idea to start with basic, "bare bones" examples of each genre. But out in the real world you might come across texts which differ somewhat from the descriptions offered here. There could be several reasons for this:

- the text might belong to a different genre not covered in this book

- the text might be a mixture of genres (we mix them all the time – sometimes deliberately for effect, sometimes carelessly because our purpose is unclear)

- the text might include additional elements not treated here

- the text might have some elements arranged in a different order.

When you are exploring a text and you want to identify its genre, skim read and try to decide what **purpose** it has been written for – to explain, to persuade, to tell what happened, and so on.

You might then ask yourself whether the text has achieved its purpose. If so, how? You might want to look first at its overall structure, asking these sorts of questions:

- What sort of focus does the text have? (A sequence focus? A "thing" focus? An argument focus? Some sort of combination?)

- What stages does the text go through? (What sort of beginning, middle and end, if any, does it have?)

- What is the function of each of these stages? (How does each contribute towards the fulfilling of the text's purpose?)

- What name could you give each stage to indicate its function?

If necessary, you could then go further into the language of the text and ask what other language features such a genre might have, e.g.

- types of participants: generalised or specific?

- tense: past or present? "timeless" or "real time"?

- personal opinions: appropriate or not?

- details: what sort are needed?

Remember that you are looking for overall patterns of language typical of the genre – not hard and fast rules. Let your commonsense guide you.

Terminology

The terminology used to refer to different aspects of texts can be a helpful tool – as long as it is meaningful to the children and not just empty jargon. You may have to decide whether to use terms developed by the class, or whether to use terms such as those suggested in this book. (Although these may seem a little daunting at first, children appear to have little difficulty with them.) But whatever choice you make, it is important that the term should give some indication of the **function** of that particular aspect of language and that the children come to an understanding of the function before attaching labels.

APPENDIX

Unhappily Ever After

Paul Jennings

Albert pulled up his socks and wiped his sweaty hands on the seat of his pants. He did up the top button of his shirt and adjusted his school tie. Then he trudged slowly up the stairs.

He was going to get the strap.

He knew it, he just knew it. He couldn't think of one thing he had done wrong but he knew Mr Brown was going to give him the strap anyway. He would find some excuse to whack Albert – he always did.

Albert's stomach leapt up and down as if it was filled with jumping frogs. Something in his throat stopped him from swallowing properly. He didn't want to go. He wished he could faint or be terribly sick so he would have to be rushed off to hospital in an ambulance. But nothing happened. He felt his own feet taking him up to his doom.

He stood outside the big brown door and trembled. He was afraid but he made his usual resolution. He would not cry. He would not ask for mercy. He would not even wince. There was no way he was going to give Mr Brown that pleasure.

He took a deep breath and knocked softly.

Inside the room Brown heard the knock. He said nothing. Let the little beggar suffer. Let the little smart alec think he was in luck. Let him think no one was in.

Brown heard Albert's soft footsteps going away from the door. "Come in, Jenkins," he boomed.

The small figure entered the room. He wore the school uniform of short pants, blue shirt and tie. His socks had fallen down again.

Albert looked over to the cupboard where the long black strap hung on a nail.

Brown towered over Albert. He wore a three-piece suit with a natty little vest. He frowned. The wretched child showed no fear. He didn't beg, he didn't cry. He just stood there.

In the corner a grandfather clock loudly ticked away the time that lay between Albert and his painful fate. The soft "clicks" of a cricket match filtered through the open window. Albert pretended he was out there playing with the others.

Brown suddenly thrust his hand into his vest pocket and pulled out a piece of paper. He pushed it into Albert's face. Somehow Albert managed to focus his eyes on it and see the words:

BALD HEAD BROWN WENT TO TOWN,

RIDING ON A PONY.

Underneath was a drawing of a bald-headed person riding a horse.

"I didn't do it, Sir," said Albert truthfully.

Brown looked at Albert's thick black hair and wiped his hand over his own bald head. The room started to swirl, his forehead throbbed. Jenkins was lying. And he was unafraid. He should be whimpering and crawling like the others.

Brown rushed over to the cupboard and grabbed the strap. "Hold out your hand," he shrieked.

Then he rained blow after blow on the helpless, shaking child.

Brown sprawled in his leather chair. He was out of breath. He knew he had overdone it this time. He had lost his temper. He wondered if Jenkins would have any bruises. Some of the other teachers might kick up a fuss if Jenkins showed them bruises. Fortunately this was a boarding school and there were no parents around to complain. Brown suddenly wished he had hit Jenkins even harder. He looked out of the window at the sparkling sea nearby. It was the perfect day to be on the water. He decided to go out in his rowing boat. It might help him to forget Jenkins and all the other little horrors in the school.

The sea was flat and mirrored the glassy clouds that beckoned from the horizon. Brown pushed out the small boat and it knifed a furrow through the inky water. He put his back to the oars and soon he was far out to sea with the shore only a thin line in the distance.

Brown was glad to be out of reach of the children he hated, but something was wrong. The sea didn't feel the same, or smell the same. He thought he heard voices – watery, giggling voices. He looked around but there was not another craft to be seen. He was alone on an enamelled ocean.

The boat began to rock gently and Brown felt it gripped in a strong current. It was carrying him away from the land. He tried to turn the boat around and pull for the shore but the current was too strong. The boat sped faster and faster and then began to rock wildly. Brown felt the oars snatched from his hands by the speeding tide. He fell with a crash to the bottom of the boat and clung to the edges as it bucketed through the swirling water.

Laughter filled the still air and echoed in his head. Brown plucked up his courage and peeped over the side of the boat. It was cutting a large circle through the foam, getting neither closer nor further away from the shore.

Suddenly a piercing pain shot through Brown's head. He just had time to notice that the sea had opened up into a large funnel. The water was twirling as if it was going down a plughole. Brown collapsed into blackness as the boat slipped over the rim of the abyss.

When he awoke the pain had gone. Brown found himself still in the boat. It was speeding around the inside of the funnel at an enormous rate. He looked up at the rim and beyond that to the clouds which spun like patterns on a drunken dinner plate.

The boat maintained its position, neither falling lower in the funnel nor rising to the surface high above. Brown peered cautiously over the edge and looked down. He gasped as he saw the spiralling funnel twist down and end in jagged claws of rock which clutched hungrily upwards from the bed of the sea.

Brown found his gaze drawn into the shining black wall of the vortex. With a shock he saw a scene unfold within the sea. Two enormous lobsters were holding a struggling, naked man over a pot of boiling water. As they dropped the figure to his death, Brown was sure he heard one of them say, "I've heard they scream as they hit the water. I don't believe it myself."

This scene repeated itself every time the boat circled. It was like a record stuck in a groove. Brown saw it a hundred times, a thousand times. It was horrible. He didn't want to watch but his eyes were held by an unseen force. Finally he grabbed the side of the boat, closed his eyes and rocked with all his strength.

The boat slipped down a few notches. When he opened his eyes another scene unfolded. A fat man sat peering through a window at a table laden with food. Trifles, jellies, cakes, peaches and strawberries. Around the table thin, ghostly children sat stuffing themselves and laughing happily. The fat man banged on the window. He was hungry. He wanted to get in. But the children couldn't see him, couldn't hear him and the man banged in vain. He was starving – never to be satisfied.

Brown watched, horrified as the same drama played again and again. Where was this place? Was it hell? Were these people having done to them what they had done to others? For ever? Over and over again?

Brown knew every groove would contain a similar horror. He could stand it no longer. He wanted to see no more. He decided to get it over and done with. He grabbed the sides of the boat and rocked and rocked and rocked. The boat plummeted to the waiting rocks below.

There was a tearing, crushing, splintering as Brown's last scream fled his tortured body.

Brown awoke and looked around. With relief he saw he was still in his study. The grandfather clock ticked away loudly in the corner and the soft "clicks" of a game of cricket filtered through the open window. His leather chair rested in its usual place.

He must have had a nightmare. For a second, but only a second, he wondered if there had been some message in his terrible dream. Then he dismissed the thought and tried to think of another excuse to give Jenkins a belting. He wasn't the least bit sorry for what he had done.

It was then he noticed the room seemed different. The grandfather clock looked taller than usual and the window appeared further from the floor. Everything was bigger. He looked down and saw he was wearing short pants. And his socks were hanging down around his shoes. He was dressed in the school uniform.

And worse – oh – much worse. Albert Jenkins was in the room. A huge Jenkins. He wore a three-piece suit with a natty little vest.

Jenkins shoved a piece of paper into Brown's face. Then he rushed over to the cupboard and grabbed the strap.

REFERENCES

Callaghan, M. and Rothery, J., *Teaching Factual Writing: A Genre Based Approach*, Report of the DSP Literacy Project, Metropolitan East Region, NSW Department of Education, Sydney, 1988.

Christie, F., *Writing in Schools*, Vol. 1 Study Guide; Vol. 2 Reader, Deakin University Press, Geelong, 1989.

Collerson, J. (ed.), *Writing for Life*, Primary English Teaching Association, Rozelle, 1988.

DSP Literacy Project, *The Report Genre*, Metropolitan East Region, NSW Department of Education, Sydney, 1989.

DSP Literacy Project, *The Discussion Genre*, Metropolitan East Region, NSW Department of Education, Sydney, 1989.

Halliday, M.A.K., *A Short Introduction to Functional Grammar*, Edward Arnold, London, 1985.

Macken, M. et al., *An Approach to Writing K-12: Introduction*, Literacy and Education Research Network, Directorate of Studies, NSW Department of Education, Sydney, 1989.

Macken, M. et al., *Factual Writing: A Teaching Unit Based on Reports about Sea Mammals*, Literacy and Education Research Network, Directorate of Studies, NSW Department of Education, Sydney, 1989.

Macken, M. et al., *Story Writing: A Teaching Unit Based on Narratives, News Stories and Fairy Tales*, Literacy and Education Research Network, Directorate of Studies, NSW Department of Education, Sydney, 1989.

Macken, M. et al., *The Theory and Practice of Genre-Based Writing*, Literacy and Education Research Network, Directorate of Studies, NSW Department of Education, Sydney, 1989.

Martin, J. and Rothery, J., *Writing Project Report*, Nos. 1, 2 and 4, Department of Linguistics, University of Sydney, Sydney, 1980, 1981, 1986.